## PRAISE FOR *THE INNOVATION ZONE*

*"Innovation is not about serendipity and chance. It's a skill and discipline that can be taught and refined.* The Innovation Zone *will teach you how the best, brightest, and most innovative companies have done just that—and it will change the way you look at innovation!"*

—CHRIS CHOLLECCI, VICE PRESIDENT,
RESEARCH VENTURES & LICENSING, PARTNERS HEALTHCARE

*"With so much hype and hope hanging on the spirit and value of innovation in these trying times, it is no small wonder that many articles and books are being written about this topic. Fortunately,* The Innovation Zone *is one of those about hope, not hype, and is critical reading for anyone or any group serious about understanding and applying innovation ideas and concepts to generate value."*

—EUGENE S. MEIERAN, SENIOR FELLOW, INTEL

*"Innovation is not a commodity.* The Innovation Zone *absolutely does not fall into this trap. It provides stories of how the best companies re-invent themselves, how they re-innovate. It emphasizes the processes they have gone through in making re-innovation a reality. Implement similar processes—appropriately—in your organization, and you're also on the road to success."*

—BOB GALLIERS, PROVOST, BENTLEY UNIVERSITY;
EDITOR-IN-CHIEF, *JOURNAL OF STRATEGIC INFORMATION SYSTEMS*

*"*The Innovation Zone *challenges conventional wisdom that innovation is something special and unique. There is no creative class in the Innovation Zone, only people who bring their experience, ideas, passion, and willingness to learn. Koulopoulos shows you how to take these and create the new solutions that drive and sustain performance and productivity."*

—MARK P. MCDONALD, GROUP VICE PRESIDENT,
GARTNER EXECUTIVE PROGRAMS

# THE INNOVATION ZONE

# THE
# INNOVATION
## ZONE

## HOW GREAT COMPANIES
## RE-INNOVATE FOR AMAZING SUCCESS

THOMAS M. KOULOPOULOS

Davies-Black Publishing
Mountain View, California

Published by Davies-Black Publishing, a division of CPP, Inc., 1055 Joaquin Road, 2nd Floor, Mountain View, CA 94043; 800-624-1765.

Special discounts on bulk quantities of Davies-Black Publishing books are available to corporations, professional associations, and other organizations. For details, contact the Director of Marketing and Sales at Davies-Black Publishing: 650-691-9123; fax 650-623-9271.

Visit the Davies-Black Publishing Web site at www.daviesblack.com.

Printed in the United States of America.
13 12 11 10 09   10 9 8 7 6 5 4 3 2 1

Library of Congress Cataloging-in-Publication Data

Koulopoulos, Thomas M.
   The innovation zone : how great companies re-innovate for amazing success / Thomas M. Koulopoulos.
      p. cm.
Includes index.
ISBN 978-0-89106-234-9 (hardcover)
1. Organizational change. 2. Creative ability. 3. Technological innovations. 4. Organizational effectiveness. 5. Success in business. I. Title.
HD58.8.K674 2009

2008034693

658.4'063—dc22

FIRST EDITION
First printing 2009

*To my father, who taught me the*
*most important lesson of innovation:*
Never give up!

# CONTENTS

# PREFACE

My professional fascination with the topic of innovation began many years ago when my friend Jim Champy first introduced me to the late management icon Peter Drucker. Drucker's matter-of-fact and very practical approach to innovation seemed to me to be in stark contrast to the sort of innovation ideology I had grown up with, which placed innovation on the top of some distant Mount Olympus in reach of only the gods and the world's greatest minds.

Over the years my interest in innovation grew as I built my own company, Delphi Group (which I later sold to a large multinational), ran a global innovation lab, and ultimately found my way back to consulting and writing. During much of that time I took untold mental notes about innovation, how it worked and how it didn't. Eventually that ended up in a capability assessment I developed and used with hundreds of organizations, as well as an appointment to run an innovation research center at Babson College, all of which finally became the foundation for this book.

Still, the lens for all of this was consistently what Drucker had taught me.

I am privileged to have had a very special and long-standing relationship with Peter. He and I met at his Claremont home several times, and he spoke at many Delphi Group events. Among many other things, over the years we discussed a wide variety of topics that have shaped and guided much of my own approach to innovation. What will always remain with me about Peter is not the greatness of his mind or the clarity of his thinking, both of which were without peer, but rather his ability to maintain focus despite the background noise that so often distracts most of us. Today I think this clarity is what we most lack when it comes to the topic of innovation.

While innovation may be the latest topic for discussion in many organizations, Drucker was a longtime proponent of ideas and concepts about innovation, which today many are rediscovering. At the core of his philosophy on the topic was a belief, which he wrote about in his 1985 book *Innovation and Entrepreneurship,* that innovation was mostly about simple, commonsense processes that needed to be put in place and made into a discipline. Drucker was nothing if not practical.

In my own work with many organizations struggling with innovation I have found this to be eminently true. We far too often overaggrandize innovation. We make it something that only the superhuman among us can achieve. We ascribe it to a mystical ability that you are either born with or acquire through some divine providence. In part we do this to take ourselves off the hook. After all, we are mere mortals; how can we be expected to be as innovative as these great minds? Nothing could be further from the truth.

I've seen innovation work in mundane and invisible ways to create the foundation for some of the most amazing success stories in this book. However, much of what passes for innovation is just the visible tip of an enormous iceberg of processes and practices. Thus no one can replicate the behaviors and the process of innovation by looking at the end result, any more than you can learn how to hit home runs by analyzing the shape of a baseball bat instead of developing an instinctive understanding of how to swing the bat, how to anticipate the pitcher, and how to play the wind and the ballpark. In the context of an organization the rules are no different. The chemistry of innovation is invisible; it cannot be understood by simply looking at the end result and trying to fast-forward to it. And the greatest of any organization's innovations is never in a specific product; it's in the innovation of the business model itself.

That, in short, is the purpose of this book, to look beyond the obvious and to understand the building blocks of innovation that must always be in place for innovation to succeed.

But there is no single approach to innovation. Instead, approaches are as numerous as organizations, cultures, and people. This is a book of stories about the way innovation takes place—stories that talk about the essential lessons and laws of innovation that we all need to learn and to teach our children in order for tomorrow's organizations, governments, and societies to adapt and deal with the tremendous uncertainty and changes to come. They are stories that I've learned from decades of working with organizations of all sizes across all industries as they try to cope with the ever-increasing demands, challenges, and opportunities of global markets.

I've tried, as best I can, to capture these stories clearly and simply so as to illustrate the cornerstones of innovation, but innovation itself is not a clear and simple matter. It requires work, consistency, and fortitude. It doesn't come cheap, but, as the saying goes, the price of not investing in it is infinitely higher.

Unfortunately that's a difficult lesson to learn. The lure of the siren song calling us to innovate and to get more creative, along with a steady mantra of how the future belongs to those with imagination, makes it seem that just being able to get creative is all that's needed. But are we any closer to understanding how to get more innovative or more creative? For the most part the answer is no. Too many people have been convinced that innovating is a matter of joining hands and singing "Kumbaya." Innovation is not a feel-good exercise. It needs to be grounded in some practical tools and methods. It needs systems and solutions. There's nothing wrong with feeling good about it—but you need something in place to keep innovation going after the singing and dancing have ended.

I've worked with and studied many organizations and individuals who, despite being mere mortals, have accomplished extraordinary feats of innovation and creativity by embracing simplicity and focusing on the mechanics of innovation rather than its glitz and charm.

Here's the bottom line: Innovation and creativity are processes. You can learn them and you can improve them. And if that sounds like sacrilege then it's time to sign up for a new religion, one that doesn't put the ability to innovate on a pinnacle but rather within arm's reach.

*Innovation and creativity are processes. You can learn them and you can improve them.*

As individuals and as organizations we need to be able to sense and interpret opportunity differently and respond to it much faster than we have in the past. Sounds simple enough, right? But are you living it?

In one of my earlier books, *Corporate Instinct,* I likened this phenomenon to that of placing your hand over a hot stove. For example, imagine yourself seated at a fancy Japanese steak house—the kind where eight to twelve people are crowded around a sizzling stovetop table. Now hold your hand out in front of you about six inches off the hot tabletop. Close your eyes and imagine how the dissipating heat would feel at that distance.

Now consider yourself as a metaphor for your company. Your hand is the company's ability to sense a new market or a shift in the market, and as a result to innovate. The heat is the intensity of that market shift. Slowly begin lowering your hand and stop when the heat is intense enough for the company to take positive innovative action.

How close did you get? Five inches? Two? Barely touching the surface? Some companies need to smell burning flesh before they take action. Even then, the action may be to figure out what the smell is—not remove the hand! The motto these companies seem to follow is, "Where there's smoke, there's a committee."

How many markets pass companies by, how many new opportunities get grabbed up by competitors, how many employees take good ideas elsewhere because their companies lack the awareness of themselves, their abilities, and their markets? In short, how many companies fail to feel the heat of the market until it's too late to innovate in their business?

*How many employees take good ideas elsewhere because their companies lack the awareness of themselves, their abilities, and their markets?*

The question that has occupied me for years is why some companies react while others are rendered helplessly numb. That's what I try to answer in this book.

Keep in mind, however, that innovation, by its nature, is built of constantly changing forces. Solving this equation for one set of variables doesn't mean that you've solved it for long. Falling into that trap, that any one approach to innovation can last long, is a sure-fire way to create the sort of rigid and unyielding organization that stifles innovation. This is why so many companies follow a natural life cycle of innovation from being at the top of their innovation game to not being able to innovate their way out of a paper bag. It's why the ranks of the Fortune 500 change so frequently; the average life span of a Fortune 500 company is less than ten years.

The other thing to keep in mind is that innovation is clearly not a new topic. The forces of globalization, the unrelenting pressures all companies face to cut costs, the acceleration of markets due to the Internet, a growing global consumer marketplace, and the mobility of capital have all fueled a new climate for innovation. But just as much to blame is our insatiable appetite as consumers for innovation. We simply expect new ideas, products, and services on a daily basis. This is the essence of what marketing guru Regis McKenna once called "The Never Satisfied Consumer."

When you buy a computer you know you'll have to upgrade in less than two years. The same applies to most of the products we use in our homes and offices. In many cases that is because of enhancements in speed, size, weight, power, or some other improvement in the product. However, thanks to the increasing impact of design on our buying habits, we will often trade in one product for another only to buy into the most current style. You need look no further than the leasing craze among automobile buyers to verify that. But the phenomenon applies equally to appliances, furnishings, and even kitchens and bathrooms. Many a DuPont Corian countertop has been swapped out for granite long before the Corian wore out, only because the kitchen fashion of the day changed. The perceived value in so much of what we purchase has shifted from function to fashion. People can and do argue about the waste that this sort of unrepenting consumerism creates, but it is a behavior we have all been conditioned to accept as natural in an age of high innovation.

From Steve Jobs to Bill Ford, innovation has become a mantra for organizations that are thriving as well as those that are striving. But it is questionable if most of us can really define innovation or describe how to create it. Can innovation actually be taught? Can innovation become a core competency? Are there rules you can follow to emulate the leading innovators and to create your own Innovation Zone?

Begin by asking yourself a simple question: Where did you learn to be innovative? If you're like most people, you never took a course on innovation. Few of us have learned to do it in any formal way. We learn innovation "on the job," when we learn it at all. The reality is that innovation is most often the result of serendipity, persistence, and lots of luck. But what if there's more? What if innovation can be taught? Guess what? It can. What if there are examples and methods you can follow? There are. The basic rules do exist, and in this book I lay them out for you.

One more thing before I begin. The ideas in *The Innovation Zone* are intended not only to help your organization but also to help you as an individual. One of the things I find most satisfying in the many opportunities I have to work with and speak to organizations trying to understand these concepts and practices is the profound impact they have on people at a very deep personal level.

We are all creative and we are all innovative, but in radically different ways. When we accept that and come to the realization that there are simple ways to apply our creativity, our own value, confidence, and faith in the future also grow. For me few things are more satisfy-ing than to see that transformation and to know that someone is just a few steps closer to achieving his or her innovative potential and stepping into the Innovation Zone.

# ACKNOWLEDGMENTS

Innovation is all about collaboration, and this book is a testimonial to that. I have many people to thank who have both shaped my thinking about innovation and shaped the content of this book. At the risk of not mentioning them all, I will try to acknowledge those who were my most important collaborators.

First, so much of my ideology about innovation comes from my valued interactions with the late Peter Drucker. Few people I've known have left me with professional memories as rich and as treasured. Peter's ideas are the bedrock for so much of our thinking about business, management, and markets. My thanks also go to Jim Champy, who first introduced me to Peter and who has, in his own unique way, provided me with much food for thought over many years. Jim and Peter share a unique quality of being able to see clearly despite a context of chaos—clarity that is sorely needed today.

Then there are all the innovators who were kind enough to take the time to share their ideas by contributing to this book and whose case studies can be found throughout. Their examples of how innovation can be done give innovation a face that my prose alone could never provide. Among these are Alph Bingham, CEO and founder of Innocentive; Gene Meieran, senior fellow at Intel; Colin Angle, cofounder and CEO of iRobot; Chris Colecchi, vice president, Partners Research and Ventures Licensing; Chet Huber, president of OnStar; Jim Birell, chief innovation officer at Precor; Darrell Rhea, CEO of Cheskin Added Value; John Gabrick, CEO of Mind Matters; Roger Garriock, VP of DIcor and one of the founders of Destination Imagi-Nation; Jane Durment, chief information officer at The Marcus Corporation; and of course my many colleagues at the Babson College Center for Business Innovation, who have provided a wonderful context for innovation.

I've been incredibly fortunate to have one of the industry's best literary agents, John Willig. John is an immovable force of nature who, once convinced of an idea, will simply not give up. I'm lucky to have him on my side! I'm also grateful to my editor at Davies-Black, Laura Lawson, who saw the early potential in *The Innovation Zone* and helped me give it life and structure. Her enthusiasm and keen eye drove me to meet every deadline (well, almost) and to re-innovate many of my own ideas. The rest of the team at Davies-Black has been just as wonderful to work with. Laura Simonds, Jill Anderson-Wilson, Rebecca Weisman, Laura Ackerman-Shaw, and Mark Chambers are consummate professionals who have demonstrated an interest in this project as well as creativity for it, which is rare but so very important in developing a book.

Finally, my thanks and admiration to my family. To my mother and father I owe deep appreciation for imbuing me with the spirit of curiosity and tenacity to pursue my dreams, and the opportunity to do so, whatever the odds. To my brother, who has the sharpest wit of anyone I know, my thanks for building the foundation that launched Delphi and for being there through all the ups and downs of growing a business. To my wife, Debbie, my undying love for her support and enthusiasm for my work and, during the long days and nights of authorship, keeping us and our family in motion. Finally, to my wonderful children, Mia and Adam, who prove to me every day the promise of innovation, the gratitude of a proud father for sharing with me the world through their creative eyes—and thereby giving me the best reason and motivation anyone could have to create a world just slightly better and more innovative than the one that was given to me.

# ABOUT THE AUTHOR

Thomas M. Koulopoulos is president and founder of Delphi Group, a Boston-based management and advisory firm. Since launching Delphi Group in 1987, Koulopoulos propelled the company to its position as an Inc. 500 company with global offices, a trusted brand, and a leading independent adviser on technology trends to large enterprise and government. He is also executive director of the Center for Business Innovation, where he oversees some of the world's leading research and thought leadership on the topic of business innovation.

# INTRODUCTION

## INNOVATION IN AN ERA OF UNCERTAINTY

I recall a discussion I had some years ago with Dee Hock, the founder of credit card behemoth VISA International, in which he said to me, "We're all playing a new game by the old rules. We just don't know what the new rules are yet." Indeed, at times it feels as though the world has moved forward by leaps and bounds while we have been standing still. The magnitude of the 2008 credit crisis in financial markets is only one indication of how much uncertainty has begun to erode our trust in systems we have long taken for granted. When the brightest minds around can't tell the oncoming light is a freight train, we begin to appreciate how unpredictable the future really is.

If you are expecting me to comfort you with the assurance that it's all an illusion or that it will somehow soon get better, sorry, I can't and I won't. It's real and it's going to get much harder to keep up with the pace of all this uncertainty and the innovation it will demand of us. To quote Yogi Berra, "The future ain't what it used to be."

Much of my thinking about the impact of uncertainty on innovation crystallized in a conversation with Peter Drucker shortly after the attacks on the World Trade Center on September 11, 2001. I asked Peter if he felt we were entering an era of uncertainty during which the level of anxiety and concern would rise significantly. His response, not unlike Dee Hock's, was not reassuring.

*"The future ain't what it used to be."*

According to Drucker, whether or not uncertainty is increasing is the wrong question. "There are periods, and we have been at the end of one," he told me, "where the same basic trends continue for a long time, and then there are transition periods. During these transitions you don't know yet what the new trends are. Uncertainty will be no greater than it was when I started work, which was in 1927, when you had a period of uncertainty and unpredictability up through World War II. Then after the 1950s, you had a period of great predictability and of great simplicity because basically every major policy decision was based on the question, Is it good for the Russians or is it good for us?" Drucker's conclusion: "We are now at the beginning of a long period of uncertainty."

What will this era of uncertainty look like? What sort of impact can we expect it to have on how we innovate? It's a mixed bag for sure. But what is clear to me is that we will need to re-innovate the very notion of innovation by leaving behind much of the baggage and legacy of what innovation has meant and how it has, and in many cases how it has not, been taught. Re-innovation is about rethinking how we create value. For example, Amazon.com fundamentally re-innovated the bookstore from the outside in by personalizing the experience of buying books. Bright Horizons re-innovated child care by bringing it to the workplace. Apple re-innovated the music industry by radically altering how both content and value are transferred between artist and consumer. Yet, what none of these companies—or the many more we will look at in the book—did was to invent the products or services upon which they built their amazing success. Bookstores, child care, and recorded music are old, mature markets that few people thought had room for amazing growth. But this is the purpose and ambition of re-innovation, and it's the story behind this book and the amazing successes we will talk about.

But first, let's look at a few key trends we need to keep in mind as a backdrop for this new era of innovation.

## Trend: Innovate More, Invent Less

First and foremost we will continue to experience mounting pressure on all industries to innovate at ever faster rates. As quality, access to talent, supply chains, pricing, and cost efficiencies all narrow into a slim band of differentiation, innovation will become a hotbed of competition. However, in many cases, this will lead to rampant invention with an emphasis on newness and quantity over value.

Open up any of the dozens of catalogs that tout new consumer products and you're bound to marvel at the flood of new, improved, just invented, one-of-a-kind, cool, and yet utterly useless gadgets on the market today. Is this really what innovation is all about? Do you need an Internet-enabled porta-potty? Or how about a device to attach your laptop to your steering wheel, complete with its own built-in heads-up display (if you're from Boston or Bangalore, don't answer)! What about a toaster to monogram your bagel? Absurd? Absolutely.

For too long we have gauged the success of the innovation economy by the increasing volume and speed with which we can move products from the shelf to the landfill! Today in the United States alone we discard more than five hundred thousand cell phones every day. It's time to change our view of innovation before we suffocate under its weight.

It seems that we have suddenly created an ability to invent beyond our wildest dreams; manufacturing is a global commodity, the Internet allows us to share ideas and to build on them in ridiculously short time frames, capital moves much more efficiently to fund new ideas, and micromarkets can easily be targeted and fulfilled with well-oiled supply chains.

As a result, we are surrounded by more useless inventions than at any other time in history. Affluence seems measured by the number of things we can accumulate and then drag to the trash bin. You only need to skim the pages of any in-flight SkyMall catalog to see the sort of ridiculous gadgetry being created. Invention is rampant. There is even a U.S. TV show called *American Inventor* that showcases the mythology of the lone genius inventor. Our culture of invention worship is the root cause of most of our confusion around innovation. The problem is that we use *invention* and *innovation* synonymously. While you need invention to get to innovation, invention on its own creates volume—not value.

## Trend: Educate for Innovation

Second, innovation is having a tremendous impact on education. As is true for just about everyone in the workforce today, my training on innovation came in bits and pieces, and even then the lessons were few and far between. I often joke that I must have been out sick on the day they taught innovation in my grade school class. Innovation was historically a mix of brute force and intuition with a dose of luck. No longer. Universities are starting to add innovation-specific offerings across disciplines, from engineering to business.

What's even more startling is the heightened emphasis on innovation methods and skills in K–12. Programs such as Destination

ImagiNation (www.idodi.org) have provided more than nine million children in twenty countries worldwide with training in innovation and creative problem solving. And Dean Kaman's FIRST robotics competition also teaches team-building and innovation skills to middle and high school students. These kids are just starting to flow into the workforce. When they arrive, their ability to innovate will make the rest of us appear to have been asleep at the wheel, if we were even in the driver's seat at all! Keep in mind that you probably can't teach people innovation any more than you can teach them good judgment, but you can teach them how others have been innovative. You can teach the tools of innovation and you can illustrate the behaviors most likely to support a culture of innovation.

No nation has the innovation edge, at least not yet. Sure, the United States is still the world's envy when it comes to higher education. While the United States may outsource in nearly every industry to the rest of the world, the rest of the world outsources education to the United States, not only by sending their students to our schools but by contracting with U.S. universities to build campuses on their soil. But our belief in the lead we have in higher education offers a false security, if any at all. Already, U.S. universities such as Weill Medical College (Cornell University), Georgetown, Carnegie Mellon, Texas A&M, Northwestern, Michigan State University, and Rochester Institute of Technology are offering classes in the Middle East.[1] This internationalization of U.S. universities is sure to dull the edge we have on education and also will slim the ranks of researchers at U.S. schools. The double whammy is something I fear we are very unprepared for.

Unlike the infrastructure and facilities, laboratories, and scientific equipment needed to train the past few generations of innovators, tomorrow's innovators will have access to all the knowledge and simulation they need at their fingertips. Innovation is really about increasing your confidence factor in predictable results from unpredictable experimentation. When experimentation was expensive very few could truly innovate. The barriers to entry included extensive R&D facilities and the ability to absorb the losses and risk that experimentation entailed. However, as experimentation became more virtual through computer-based simulation it also grew far less risky, and in some cases, except for the time expended, free! It's like creating a casino where the chips are piled up for the taking, available to everyone who steps through the door, but the payouts are real. Anyone is welcome to play at this table, and the card game is barely five minutes old.

## Trend: Personalize Through Innovation

Third and last, the greatest impact of innovation in the next few years will be the change it creates in the nature of personalization. In the end, markets can only be as rich in diversity, options, and innovations as buyers are in their preferences. Consumers already have the ability to order personalized clothing from Lands' End, personalized footwear from Nike, even personalized nutrition bars. This will quickly extend to every aspect of our lives.

This is where innovation will most dramatically alter the behaviors of markets, and perhaps where the brightest light on the innovation horizon is just starting to shine. Innovation has always been about creating products and services that attract the largest number of interested buyers. This is the cornerstone of mass markets. However, as innovation has accelerated we've consistently shortened the useful life of each new innovation. This may increase the rate at which products and services turn over in the market, but it's a fundamentally inefficient way to address the true needs of each consumer and the way in which a product or service adds true meaning to a buyer's life. Personalization is where innovation takes on a new dimension that simply has no parallel in today's market. We may talk about "markets of one," but we've hardly delivered on the vision. When we do, innovation will finally be driven by the market.

The challenges are there, but so are the opportunities. Vast new global markets and prosperity will open up through this new era of innovation.

## Innovating Innovation

It's easy to discount the speed and the ease with which we will shift into this new innovation-based economy. As Drucker was fond of saying, "What killed the sail [ship] was not the steamship but the fact that it takes five to eight years to train a sailor, and it takes five to eight days to train somebody to shovel coal."

The longer I look at the rate at which younger generations are already adopting the new tenets of innovation through online social networks and mass collaboration, and fundamentally changing their attitudes about what innovation is and how it should be approached, the more convinced I am that the chains that bind us to old ideas of innovation are much more fragile than we want to admit.

A new future for innovation clearly awaits us. It is not the sort of innovation we have become accustomed to, one focused on products, but rather one focused on new business models that extract greater value from social networks, collaboration, and process. It's not here yet—but it will arrive much faster than we expect. In the interim we'll scurry about trying to make sense of the commotion, looking for a way to understand it and to move forward. I have no doubt that we will get there; we always do, although perhaps not in the way we had expected. What's clear is that the discussion about innovation has to become much broader than just a discussion of products. Businesses themselves must be innovative. The twentieth-century notion of organizations and business models has no more secure place in the twenty-first century than the nineteenth-century model did in the twentieth century. Defining the new model is our job and the purpose for this book, to understand not just how to innovate products and services but how to innovate innovation itself.

CHAPTER **1**

# UNEXPECTED POSSIBILITIES

*Innovation always takes us by surprise. When the first Motorola brick-sized cell phones were introduced in 1983, the most ambitious projections were for 50 million phones in use in the year 2008. However, in 2008, more than 3.3 billion cell phones are in use around the globe. How could we consistently be so wrong about the future?*

Every time we encounter massive change, such as that brought on by cell phones, it's nearly impossible to fully appreciate the true nature of the change or the way in which it will alter our behavior. That's the reason humanity has such a miserable track record of predicting the true impact of innovation and change on the future. Thomas Watson, founder of IBM, is reported to have said that the worldwide market for computers would never exceed five. True or not, this statement always sticks in my mind as a great metaphor for how even the most visionary among us are stymied by the unpredictability of the future!

Whether it's the printing press, the automobile, the computer, or the cell phone, the human ability to find applications for new ideas and react to and adapt to change is a constant source of amazement. It is ultimately the most encouraging and optimistic aspect of human nature.

Part of the reason it is so difficult to project the path of innovation is that big change rarely comes in singular form. The impact of innovation is not predictable like the trajectory of a cannonball—it's more like the shape of a dust storm. Massive change is accompanied by a context of uncertainty, with so many forces interacting in chaotic ways that they defy any reasonable person's ability to project how the chaos will evolve.

> *The impact of innovation is not predictable like the trajectory of a cannonball—it's more like the shape of a dust storm.*

Today the changes we are experiencing in the world are many. Global markets are responding in near unison to economic and political threats and opportunities. Financial markets worldwide have been rocked by mistrust and doubt. The growing ranks of consumers are stressing industry and ecology. The empowerment of massive new pools of well-educated knowledge workers is creating unprecedented mobility of work. The number of college graduates worldwide has increased to more than 30 percent of the population in developed countries.[1] Going forward it is expected that over the next twenty years demand for higher education will increase 300 percent globally. On the other hand, the looming and amorphous threat of terrorism creates a constant undercurrent that we have barely begun to factor into our psychology.

It's an overwhelming cocktail of change. We've built organizations, economies, and societies that seem to have exceeded our ability to keep pace with our ability to innovate.

Part of the problem is that we are at the tail end of an era focused almost entirely on the innovation of products and services, and we are just at the beginning of a new era that focuses on the innovation of business models. This goes beyond just asking how we can make what we make better and cheaper or asking how we can do what we do faster. It is about asking why we do something to begin with. When Apple created iTunes it didn't just create a faster, cheaper, better digital format for music; it altered the very nature of the relationship between music and people. eBay did not just create a market for auctions; it changed the way in which we look at the very experience of shopping and how community plays a role in the experience. When GM created OnStar it didn't just make getting from point A to point B faster; it changed the relationship between auto manufacturer and buyer and fundamentally altered the reasons for buying a car. Dell did not create personal computers, but it radically changed the way people build and buy them. Google did not invent Internet search, but it changed the way advertisers find and pay for buyers.

These are all examples of business model innovation: obvious in themselves, but obviousness is the foundation of every great innovation. However, until recently business model innovation occurred infrequently. The change in today's world and in the future will be that the innovation of our businesses will need to be as continuous a process as the innovation of products has been over the past hundred years.

*We are just at the beginning of a new era that focuses on the innovation of business models.*

Of course, it will continue to be important to innovate products and services, but it's not enough to simply acknowledge product innovation. We need to rethink innovation to include the way we define and redefine our businesses. We need to think of products and services as the outcome of a process of continuous business innovation. It's here that the greatest payback and value of innovation will be found, but they have yet to be fully understood and exploited. We are stuck in an old model of innovation. So to help set aside old ways of thinking about innovation, let me begin by first defining what innovation is not.

First, innovation is not invention. It's not about creating the next new gadget, wonder drug, or weapon. Innovation is not about accelerating the rate at which we create stuff; it's about accelerating the rate at which we create *value*. Innovation cannot exist in the absence of value that is recognized and rewarded. Invention can. Patent and trademark files are filled with inventions that never created any value. Innovation is not invention run amuck.

Second, innovation is not a slogan or a mantra—a vessel into which we can pour old wine—just to create the illusion of faster, cheaper, better. Innovation is about change that matters, change that creates a new experience; it's about changing behavior. Innovation is about altering the context of our lives and creating possibilities no one has dreamed of—not just an idea that sits on a shelf.

*Innovation is a process of change with measurable value.*

Simply put, *innovation is a process of change with measurable value.* If you keep that in mind as you read this book, you'll have a compass setting that helps you understand the ways in which you can harness innovation.

## INNOVATION VERSUS INVENTION

**Invention is an event.** It

- Requires little effort
- Occurs in an instant of time
- Provides discrete and autonomous ideas
- Typically leads to little long-term value
- Focuses on products and not processes

**Innovation is more—it's a process.** It

- Provides measurable value
- Requires sustained investment and nurturing
- Alters behavior and culture
- Causes fundamental changes in a business and processes, not just a product or service

Most important, keep in mind that innovation is about dealing with uncertainty in all its forms, good and bad. The more innovative you are, the more likely you are to survive and thrive in the future. That's not a mandate for your next best product; it's a mandate for your business in the face of the unknown.

## The Nature of Innovation

Innovation is steeped in and intimately tied to uncertainty. We cannot predict what we cannot know. What we can do is prepare ourselves to deal with the unknown when it arrives. It's what I call the *uncertainty principle;* namely, as the world moves faster and becomes less predictable, our windows of opportunity to respond become ever smaller. Opportunity doesn't go away; in fact it increases, but each opportunity lasts for less time. That is perhaps the most daunting and intimidating aspect of innovation: its relentless progress toward increasingly faster-moving targets. For many of us, the idea of innovation as an endless series of unplanned

*We cannot predict what we cannot know. What we can do is prepare ourselves to deal with the unknown when it arrives.*

explorations into the unknown with unknown return is difficult to grasp and justify.

The future is periodically shaped by things that do not yet exist. And the solutions we need will develop in response to problems that also don't yet exist. For example, think of how many of the jobs in today's organizations even existed fifty years ago. How many new positions will we create for the organizations of tomorrow?

I'm trying to point out how absurd it is to expect that the future is just a continuation of the past. Think of the sea change in attitudes toward ecology that resulted from the view of a fragile blue marble-like Earth as seen for the first time from the Apollo moon missions. We can look back with much greater clarity on the moment the world changed, and when the challenges of the future were created, than we ever could looking forward. Unfortunately, when we ask ourselves how innovation will shape the future, we are forever stuck in the past.

## Generations of Innovation

People of many ages work side by side in today's organizations, blurring generational lines. They use vastly different lenses through which to view innovation, and these views divide generations better than tie-dyed jeans and Pink Floyd ever did. Understanding these differences in perspective is critical in applying the basic principles of innovation to an organization.

### THE APOLLO GENERATION

How old were you when a man first landed on the moon? If you can answer that question, you are part of the generation that is stuck in the last century of innovation. I'm part of that generation. I call us Apollos, named after the space program that put the first man on the moon. Like the footprints of astronauts that are still, and will be for millennia, clearly marked on the lunar surface, many of us are stuck in time. Sure, we may have moved on in terms of keeping up with the latest technologies, and we have all certainly learned new things, but that's not what I'm referring to. We are stuck in terms of how we understand the mechanics of innovation.

What if I were to tell you that innovation is, as John Lennon said about life, "what happens to you when you're busy making other plans"? What if innovation were more about dealing with uncertainty than predictability? If you're an Apollo, does this sit well with you? Probably not. It's not the way we Apollos have been taught to think. After all, the better you can predict the future, the better you can tell what needs to be innovated. This is what Drucker meant by working in periods of prolonged predictability. But that only applies if you believe that the future is simply a continuation of the past and somehow the result of only the experiences you have had to date. And as we've seen, it's not.

When I speak to executives or address large audiences I can instantly spot the Apollos. All I need to do is look at their faces when I talk about uncertainty. Apollos like to set an objective for a known problem. They are obsessively objective driven. They hate to invest without a firm and unequivocal objective in mind. No surprise there—it's the way we learned to approach the biggest challenges of our age. We knew our enemies. In war it was clear who we were fighting against. Either you were one of our allies or you were the enemy. In the cold war you were a communist or you were not. In the space race either you set foot on the moon or you didn't. You were a flower child or you were "the man." The world was black and white.

## THE "NOW" GENERATION

The current generation couldn't care less about the objective. Their joy and passion is in exploring with no definite end in mind. It's why so many of them put so much time into social networking sites like Facebook and MySpace with no definite return. The joy for them is in the social journey, not the destination. It has to be; their world has become a continuous spectrum of gray with few stark contrasts. Terrorism is amorphous and insidious, with no single geographic border or national enemy. Economies are merging in vast global coalitions, sometimes explicitly, as is the case with the European Community, and in other cases implicitly, as in Asia and Latin America.

## THE JOURNEY FROM ART TO SCIENCE

Understanding how innovation is changing and how we can build it into our businesses, attitudes, schools, and very culture requires rethinking much of what we've been taught and have experienced about invention and innovation. We need to look beyond the glitz to the tools, processes, and behaviors that create value through innovation. We need to build the skills of innovation into our organizations and our leaders. Most important, we need to figure out ways to sustain innovation and create enduring value rather than the periodic flash in the pan that has typified innovation to date.

The good news is we have no choice. You need not ponder the call to be more innovative as if it were being posed as a question. Today's global markets and global challenges are far too complex to allow for the option of standing still. We need a new set of rules for *business innovation* in marketing, processes, and partnership—now.

## The Five Laws of Innovation

I call the basic new truths the Five Laws of Innovation: the immutable laws followed by every organization that is able to sustain innovation for any reasonable period of time.

### THE FIVE LAWS OF INNOVATION

- Innovation is dangerous.
- Innovators are impervious to rejection.
- Innovation is not invention.
- Innovation is not a solo flight.
- Innovation is *always* a threat to yesterday's success.

These laws apply equally to how we innovate products and businesses. However, organizations that live by these rules don't see a distinction between the innovation of a product, a service, or a whole business. Innovation for them becomes a process that results in whatever is best suited for translating their ideas into value.

### INNOVATION IS DANGEROUS

Innovation is dangerous, so *go where the fear is.* Have no illusions about this. If you want to be an innovator, you have to look at risk differently from most people. Innovators embrace risk as an ally; they look for risk as an indicator of where others fear to go—and then they go there themselves. They are not always the first to go; in fact they rarely are, but they are astute observers and they learn from the risks others have taken on the same path.

*We endlessly attempt to convince ourselves that the only correct view is the one we have been taught and subsequently taught to others.*

History is littered with examples of innovation in the face of the immutable. It is human nature that we put up barriers to protect the great ideas in which we have already invested so heavily, both mentally and financially. We fail to see, however, that these same ideas we try so hard to protect went through the identical processes of overcoming the immutable ideas that preceded them. Like Ptolemy and Copernicus, we endlessly attempt to convince ourselves that the only correct view is the one we have been taught and subsequently taught to others. Why not? It makes perfect sense that our very identity and the pride in our own intellect would prevent us from adopting a radical idea we ourselves have not been able to create.

If you're finding this a bit hard to believe, look around yourself right now. I bet there are at least a good half dozen innovations within reach that have so changed your life and how you behave that you cannot recall what life was like before them. A cell phone, a laptop, an ATM, wireless global Internet access, GPS, an artificial organ or an implant, e-mail, instant messaging. The list can be found in every nook and cranny of modern life. So how often do you find yourself asking, "How did I get along without [fill in the blank]?" Now ask yourself why that same innovation was rejected by the market and industry before it became so indispensable. I'll guess it's easier to recall what life was like before it than to recall why it wasn't so obvious.

Yet we constantly fall into the same trap by attaching ourselves too closely to *what is* and distancing ourselves from *what can be*. It's not because we don't appreciate the power of a cell phone but rather that we can't appreciate how, over time, it will change the way we behave. New behaviors open the door to new business opportunities, which is where radical innovation begins.

Organizations also fall into the trap of fearing innovation and what it may require them to reveal to their partners and in many cases competitors. The reason is that many innovations have little if any impact unless they are shared across partners and throughout an industry. Take, for instance, technologies such as Bluetooth that are widely used in computers and cell phones for wireless connectivity.

This sort of innovation is distinctly different from the sort of invention that characterized the early part of the twentieth century, when ownership and products were both much simpler and more straightforward. The paranoia of these early models of invention lingers in the way many organizations continue to approach innovation.

The problem is that innovation in every industry is moving from an ownership model to a strategic model, as shown in Figure 1. This model requires innovation of the processes of cooperation across competitors. Few industries enable a single company to own all the pieces needed to get from idea to market. Yet innovations that threaten to change a model across an industry are almost always seen as extremely dangerous to the existing relationship with customers and the proprietary efforts of each competitor to serve its customers in a way that differentiates it from the pack. These same differentiators can create extreme frustration on the part of the customers, whose experience is complicated by a different set of processes and services each time they deal with a different provider.

FIGURE 1. **THE TWENTIETH-CENTURY SHIFT IN ORGANIZATIONS**

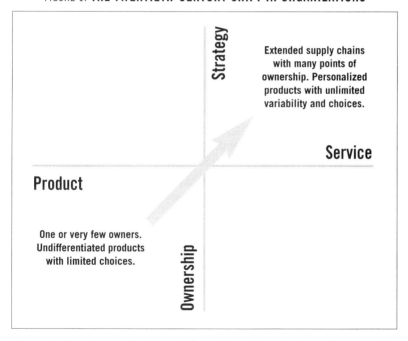

*Companies have been undergoing a shift over the past hundred years from organizing around products and ownership to organizing around strategy and service. This is the model I created after a conversation with Peter Drucker on the topic of organizational change during the twentieth century. In the upper right quadrant organizations are tasked with innovation for a market that requires nearly infinite variability of products and services spread across many parts of their value chain.*

For example, take the hotel and hospitality industry, which involves an intricate network of suppliers, complex ownership relationships, and a very diverse set of services. Dozens of different and disconnected systems are involved in managing a hotel guest's stay. Every time you stay at a hotel, information about your stay is captured in myriad transactions: reservations, check-in, room service, movies, Internet access, restaurant, health club, spa, transportation, preferences, complaints, interactions at the front desk and checkout, and probably more.

Yet answer this: When was the last time you checked into a hotel and were greeted by someone at the front desk who knew your name, preferences, and itinerary without knowing you personally? I've lived much of my life on the road, staying at countless hotels, and yet it has never happened to me. With a name like Koulopoulos you would think it unlikely that I'd wind up being confused with too many other guests. But with all that data about me floating around in nearly every major hotel chain, not once has someone said to me, "Welcome back, Mr. Koulopoulos! We have your king bed with an extra fluffy pillow, a bottle of sparkling water, and classical music programmed into your 6:30 alarm, and by the way the Discovery Channel has a documentary this evening on one of your favorite subjects. Enjoy your night with us and have a safe trip tomorrow to our next hotel in Anytown." Okay, maybe I'm dreaming a bit, but what I do get in most cases is more along the lines of, "Hi, Mr. Kalappopallopaloiz. Could you fill in your name, address, and phone number? By the way, have you stayed with us before?"

The problem faced by hotels is in the complexity of the systems used to track all this data and the lack of integration among them. The solution here is not found in any single hotel system but rather in changing the way the industry works. Until recently that was a long shot in this highly competitive industry, but things are beginning to change. A new nonprofit called Hotel Technology Next Generation (HTNG) has been formed by competing hotel groups such as Starwood, Marriott, Hyatt, and Intercontinental, along with suppliers and independent hotel management companies such as The Marcus Corporation based in Wisconsin. HTNG's mission is simple: revamp the business model of the hotel industry to provide customer-centered innovations. It's a simple idea but enormously difficult to jump-start in the face of the outdated but still prevalent model of innovation as something only one company owns.

According to Jane Durment, chief information officer at The Marcus Corporation and herself a board member of HTNG, "This approach provides a key innovation for the hospitality industry since it creates a common guest understanding among competitors and the entire hospitality supply chain." Durment foresees a day in the near future when you will open your hotel room door to find the room completely personalized, no matter where you are or how often you have been there. Not only will your accommodations be personalized but your TV will have your favorite channels and movies in your native language, and your food preferences, spa treatments, wake-up times, transportation requirements, itinerary, even the temperature of the water in your shower may all be set up based on your preferences.

*Do competitive concerns outweigh the customer value that can be delivered through competitive collaboration?*

The application of customer-centered innovation of this sort extends across many other industries as well. Still, it is an uphill battle. The question ultimately is, Do competitive concerns outweigh the customer value that can be delivered through competitive collaboration? Customers naturally have their own vantage point on that, while providers try to hold onto the vestiges of a proprietary process and offerings. Overcoming the fear and danger of moving forward frequently requires help from an outside entity, such as HTNG, that can bring together the critical mass of the industry to innovate across its internal boundaries. The result for this industry is typically an increase in overall customer satisfaction and a higher level of service that creates growth for all players. Think of the computer industry of the past ten years, which has exploded in large part due to the common platform of the Internet.

## INNOVATORS ARE IMPERVIOUS TO REJECTION

Innovators are impervious to rejection, *so hang in there*. If you want to be an innovator, get ready for a whole lot of convincingly articulate people to tell you why you are wrong: very wrong, desperately wrong, misguided, and in need of professional help. They will be your friends, your colleagues and employees, even your family. They will mean well. They will convince themselves of your folly, and you will be able to do nothing to change their minds until you succeed. If you want to innovate, get used to it; if you innovate enough, they *might* get used to you!

Sometimes it's necessary to find the conviction to stand your ground with unwavering certainty. What I'm referring to here is not the irrational stubbornness of people who dig in their heels and refuse to budge simply because they want to continue doing things the way they have always been done, but rather the persistence of those who have a vision of how things can be done differently. I know this sounds like a very fine line, perhaps even just a difference of words. After all, how is stubbornness different from conviction of vision? The two are often one and the same, and sometimes they are opposite sides of the same coin, acting as the innovator's greatest asset and nemesis.

*Something about an organization of even moderate scale tends to drive innovation into hiding.*

The difference between stubbornness and conviction lies in the degree to which the holder is moving forward as opposed to looking backward. As my friend Glenn Mangurian, who wrote an article on the topic for the *Harvard Business Review,* is fond of saying, "It's a whole lot easier to build new dreams than to repair old ones."[2] Innovators are always in the process of building new dreams. They have little attachment to old ones, even those once very successful. In part this makes them appear scattered and unorthodox to those around them. But their ability to consistently and successfully leapfrog old ideas ultimately creates an aura of success that draws people to them. Ironically, their success often leads to the creation of organizations that eventually develop their own antibodies to innovation. Something about an organization of even moderate scale tends to drive innovation into hiding. And it's not merely a matter of unnecessary bureaucracy and politics; my experience has taught me that a very real fear of rejection develops in both individuals and organizations.

From the individual's point of view, the problem is fear of rejection of a new idea by superiors. People become conditioned to keeping quiet unless they can demonstrate the payback: "Better to keep your mouth shut and let people think you're a fool than to open it and prove them right!" That's also the reason so many ideas are quickly co-opted by others when they do start to take root. It's not that people maliciously steal an idea; they simply come to recognize it and are drawn to participate in something that has crossed the barrier of acceptance.

While heightened levels of online collaboration may seem to create more opportunities for ideas to be plagiarized by others, online collaboration also offers a very distinct counterbalance to plagiarism. Online systems create new levels of transparency. The ability to document the actual creator of an idea by tracing its digital signature, or the trail left behind in various online communication channels and databases, is making the processes of co-opting harder to pull off.

From an organizational standpoint, companies also fear the market's punishment for taking on new ideas, which are inherently risky. This is the reason large companies are often stifled in their eagerness to innovate. Financial markets have become notorious for focusing tightly on the next quarter's earnings and forecasts. So much energy is expended on them that very little is left over to innovate. *Strategy* and *innovation* become words in a corporate mission statement or a list of values, but the activities they represent rarely appear in the day-to-day battle in the trenches.

## INNOVATION IS NOT INVENTION

Innovation is not invention, so *take the long view*. We often invent things just because we can, not because they have any utility or value. The result is that, unfortunately, we try to measure innovation by how quickly we can move product from the shelf to the landfill. It seems that the quicker we can do that, the more stuff we can throw away, the more innovative we believe we have become. That's not innovation.

Remember, innovation is about creating value. It is about doing something that truly is going to enhance the human condition and that will somehow add greater meaning to our lives. If we use that as our compass setting for innovation, we are going in the right direction.

However, if we continue on our current path of rampant invention, the result will be interesting from an academic standpoint—but I'm afraid it may add thousands of tons of slightly used and quickly outdated gadgetry to the ecosystem. The world is already reeling from decades of innovation in plastics and electronics that will be biodegrading in landfills for the next hundred millennia. And the worst is probably yet to come.

The bottom line here is that we need to become as adept at innovating in the way we dispose of our good ideas as we are at creating them. It's not that there is anything wrong with inventing. We are all inventors; we have to be to survive the uncertainty of even the most mundane life. Inventing is a natural part of the human condition.

*Unfortunately, we try to measure innovation by how quickly we can move product from the shelf to the landfill.*

It's just that we often ignore the process of getting from invention to value. For example, think of the last time you opened up a catalog or shopped in a store and saw something that caused you to say to yourself, "Hey, I had that idea. If I had followed through, I could have made millions on it." Sure, but was it the idea that created the value or the ability to get it from mind to market? Clearly most ideas never make it beyond the warm and moist confines of the gray matter that gives birth to them. We all have extraordinary ideas. What we lack in that brief moment of jealousy is the appreciation for the amazingly complex series of tasks required to commercialize the idea. And organizations face the same problem: Ideas exist in abundance in the experiences and wisdom of every employee, but it is no simple matter to cultivate these ideas in a manner that puts them into practice.

The reality is that we all are fascinated with invention, but few of us have been taught how to sustain innovation, and fewer still want to put in the effort that it takes. We give up on our ideas too fast and then we grieve over their carcasses for too long. Anyone can invent. We all have the same basic resources to come up with new ideas. The question is, Are you willing and able to sustain the good idea as it grows, or can your organization do this for its employees? The analogy I like to use is parenthood. Any dope can participate in the conception of a child, give birth to it, and feed it and watch it grow. It doesn't take much more than the basic machinery nature has provided us with to get that far. No testing, license, certification, or education needed. But being a parent involves much more. And being a good parent, well, let's just say it's a relentless process, as is innovation.

> *We give up on our ideas too fast and then we grieve over their carcasses for too long.*

## INNOVATION IS NOT A SOLO FLIGHT

Innovation is not a solo flight, *so don't try to go it alone.* I was taught that one person could change the world. I believed it, and I still do. But as I was busy trying to change the world, something else happened. The world got very, very big, uncertain, and awfully complex. And that's where solo flights began to take a back seat to team acts.

I've long suspected this to be the case. But then I began doing a bit of research on my own, and what I found has me looking at this with a whole new appreciation for the importance of teams.

Take a simple example. If you split the past century into two halves and tally up the number of Nobel prizes awarded in the physical sciences, you uncover something that's a bit startling. In the first fifty years of the twentieth century, thirty-nine Nobel prizes were awarded to individuals and four to teams. In the second fifty years, thirty-three were awarded to individuals as opposed to thirty-six for teams.

Yet more evidence of the rise of teams came from an article in *Science,* "The Increasing Dominance of Teams in Production of Knowledge."[3] After researching 19.9 million (not a typo) scientific papers written over a period of fifty years, along with 2.1 million patents, the authors uncovered a distinct and significant trend toward teams in new discovery. In fact the data are so compelling that in some areas the trend lines indicate that by 2020 scientific and engineering discoveries will result almost exclusively from team efforts.

Surprised? None of us should be. But still it's a bit like a brick over the head. Time to wake up. It's a different world and it needs different skills. Today's problems are just too big to solve single-handedly. It's funny, though. I see grown-ups who talk about teamwork but are happy only if they are at the top of the team. It can't work that way. We need to learn some drastically new behaviors and embrace new tools.

We have adopted the perverse notion that innovation is about one person's genius. We like to chalk it up to brilliant solo acts. Again, it is just human nature to look for a leader and to pin success on an individual. While it may be true that invention often starts with one person's idea and needs a leader to support it, innovation requires the chemistry and sustainability of collaboration. In fact the process of innovation, when it is most successful, extends beyond the traditional confines of the organization to include the market it serves.

*One of the hardest but most consistently important things to do when you innovate is to let the market take ownership.*

One of the hardest but most consistently important things to do when you innovate is to let the market take ownership. Think about some of the greatest innovations in your personal experience and I'll bet you feel a sense of ownership in the products. It's the way I feel about my Apple laptop. (Although if you're a PC user, you may not share my sentiment!) There is a saying that a good book is not read by you; rather, *it reads you.* Somehow the line between reader and character blurs. In this same way great innovations strike a chord deep inside us, releasing new behaviors and attitudes that somehow feel already familiar. It doesn't take long for us to get attached to the innovation, or for it to attach to us, creating an intellectually intimate relationship. Sounds a bit odd, I agree. But think of the many ways that products and services become integrated with your life and you get a sense of what I'm talking about. Opening up innovation to a team of participants, inside and outside the organization, is critical to sustaining innovation.

Perhaps the best example of how collaborative innovation has started to pervade our lives is in the example of what's popularly called Web 2.0 and open source computer software. Web 2.0 is a catchy term for the new collaborative communities forming on the Web to create amazing levels of high-quality content. For example, Wikipedia, the Internet-based encyclopedia, has by its own account more than three million articles—created entirely by volunteers. Wikipedia rivals traditional encyclopedias in both volume and accuracy of content. However, where it excels is in its timeliness. New entries and updates to Wikipedia happen in near real time, something that no traditional encyclopedia could ever do. With its global contributors it is amazingly self-policing. Articles with profanity, bias, poor documentation of facts, plagiarism, or inconsistencies are on average corrected within thirty minutes! No amount of editorial support could accomplish the feat without the vast collaborative behind Wikipedia.

In the same way, open source computer software such as Linux has become a substantial threat to products developed by major developers such as Oracle and SAP. While these companies have poured untold billions into their products, open source software is developed and continuously updated by programmers around the globe and then made available at no cost to anyone who wants to use it. Again the integrity, sophistication, and reliability of open source has dumbfounded traditional software developers, who believed that only huge organizations could develop these sorts of complex programs.

The fact is simply undeniable: Collaborative innovation—or *co-innovation*, as it's also known—is fast becoming an essential aspect of how we develop new ideas. And it is also an economically attractive and viable alternative to traditional innovation.

By the way, don't confuse collaborative innovation with a headless organization. Leadership still plays a critical role in mobilizing and aligning any organization. But the role of the leader is not to create the innovation but to create an environment in which it will thrive. Ultimately, we are drawn to individuals who can articulate the vision, mission, and intent of an organization. We are individuals and we relate best to other individuals. That's human nature and that won't change.

## INNOVATION IS *ALWAYS* A THREAT TO YESTERDAY'S SUCCESS

Innovation is always a threat to yesterday's success, *so don't get too comfortable.* Thinking about innovation, it's necessary to look back at what has already been innovated and use it as the benchmark for how wonderful innovation is. Unfortunately this gives us a very warped perception. It's tough to go back after any big innovation and recall what life was like before it. We forget the challenge of innovation as our behavior changes. Eventually those who can remember just end up being considered whiners. It is the nature of every big innovation that it is initially considered crazy, absurd, faddish, expensive, risky, and just plain silly. Innovation always threatens to displace incumbents who have big stakes in the status quo.

Innovation retools the way we behave and changes the familiar. After the fact, we forget how many people bet against it. Counterintuitive as it sounds, if you try to innovate by pleasing the market, you fail. Markets only know what they have experienced. Innovation changes experience.

*If you try to innovate by pleasing the market, you fail.*

It's not coincidence that nearly every great innovation is preceded by numerous half-hearted attempts to change an existing product incrementally and call it innovative. Markets have an amazing ability to see through this, but they don't know what they want until they get it. Early movers who try to pour old wine into new bottles convince themselves that the market's reaction is further evidence that there is no appetite for the innovation. But when markets finally get a taste of innovation, they devour it.

Although it's easy to point to examples where these challenges have been overcome, each time we approach an innovation apex the same challenges reappear. It's as though we are destined to relive the same obstacles to innovation each time we near it. But such is the nature of innovation. No matter how steep the incline and how high the last peak, another, even steeper and higher, always looms ahead. We fail to grasp the infinity of possibilities when it comes to our own creativity, and we teach our children the same failure.

One of the most astoundingly simple examples is the rise of Zipcar as an alternative to car ownership for urban dwellers who prefer to use a car periodically but don't have the benefit of a parking space nor the desire to maintain, insure, and pay for a full-time car. Traditionally the only option if you were in this position was to rent a car. But a few days of rental quickly added up to a monthly car payment and still did not solve the problem of parking in congested urban areas. Rental cars also require that you go to a central location to pick up and drop off the car. The Zipcar solution is elegantly simple but a complete departure from the old model of car ownership. Zipcar effectively provides fractional ownership in new cars. You pay a monthly fee or an hourly rate and then have access to hundreds of cars with prepaid parking and gas at dozens of city parking spots and garages. Just locate the closest car via the Web or by phone and wave your Zipcard across the window; the car unlocks, and you get in and drive. No insurance, maintenance, or registration. And, by the way, drive in a new and very urban chic car ideal for city driving.

*If you are always thinking "product," you will inevitably get stuck in the model of the product as it has existed.*

So why didn't someone think of that earlier? Well, they did, just not in the case of cars. Fractional ownership of vacation homes, aircraft, boats, and country clubs is nothing new. But in the case of cars, it simply was not part of the conventional wisdom. Herein lies one of the most important lessons in creating an Innovation Zone that truly emphasizes processes instead of products. When you combine advances in GPS, the Web, insurance costs for twenty-somethings, and the rising cost of automobiles you set the stage for an entirely new business model. If you are always thinking "product," you will inevitably get stuck in the model of the product as it has existed. The longer the product has been around, and the more successful its business model has been, the harder it is to derail your thinking and move on to a new business model. But if you look at other products and ask how they use alternative business models to meet new needs, you will soon find that innovation is far removed from the traditional product and invention model.

Zipcar certainly didn't invent the automobile, and it didn't invent the idea of fractional ownership. But it did combine them to create an entirely new business model. As you look at the examples of innovation throughout this book, don't let the product overshadow the deeper change in the business. If you learn to innovate the business model and make it part of your business, the product innovation will always follow.

The examples of innovating business models and processes as well as the lessons to be learned are plentiful and can be emulated. The past century is overflowing with cases of innovation, people and companies that dramatically changed the way we behave in and experience the world. Innovation may once have been impossible to teach, but no longer. This generation needs to learn the tools and the methods of innovation as much as the previous generation needed to know the basics of economics and finance.

## Why an Innovation Zone?

Before going much further I should answer a basic question: Why an "Innovation Zone"? The term *Innovation Zone* has a very specific meaning in this book. An Innovation Zone is a protected space within an organization, an industry, or even a geographic region where ideas are identified, evaluated, nurtured, and developed in order to create value. It's a place where free thinking is encouraged and rewarded, where the status quo is constantly challenged and redefined. The ideas developed in an Innovation Zone need not be product ideas and most often are not. They can just as easily be ideas about how to enhance or create new processes or business models. They may be ideas about how to better market or sell something, or how to combine practices from outside industries, as in the case of the Zipcar. They can even be ideas about how to better innovate. Whatever the case, these ideas often need more than just an owner; they need a place to call home while they take shape. They need a fair and objective third party to nurture and shepherd them. They need to be evaluated and inventoried. Ultimately they need to be translated into value.

But don't make this too complex. Think about the idea of an Innovation Zone in very simple terms. If someone in your organization comes up with an idea that applies to any aspect of the organization, where does he or she go with it? Think before you answer, because

*An Innovation Zone is a protected space where the status quo is constantly challenged and redefined.*

the obvious choices are often not going to get that idea too far. First, consider that I asked about *anybody*—not just senior-level individuals, but any individual. Second, consider that I asked about an idea that may apply to *any aspect* of the organization, not just the discipline or department of the idea's originator or the products and services of the organization. The problem is that while many ideas can take root in the local workgroup or department in which they originate, many more have no place to go because the organizational structure isolates them and withholds resources needed to evaluate and nurture them.

At Microsoft, for example, an idea may surface in many ways. Microsoft's internal Idea Exchange allows any employee to submit an idea, which is then voted on by other employees. Ideas that get enough attention are evaluated and moved forward. Those that aren't are archived for future reference. Microsoft also holds two yearly Think Weeks during which any employee or group of employees can write a white paper on a new idea for a product, service, or business that is reviewed by the top leadership along with the Microsoft Fellows and Microsoft Distinguished Scientists. The white papers are discussed and evaluated openly. Executives can also post challenges on an intranet and solicit ideas for solutions from any employee. All of these represent a basic effort at putting in place an Innovation Zone where ideas can flourish.

IBM has a similar initiative called ThinkPlace, which acts as an electronic sandbox, according to IBM CIO Mark Hennessey. ThinkPlace is an online Innovation Zone where anyone across the company can submit ideas and build an online dialogue around them, which in time develops the idea. Some ideas flourish and turn into innovations. Others may not make it that far, but the process is open to anybody who wants to participate.

So, simply put, an Innovation Zone provides a space where ideas can take root in fertile soil, protected from the elements of organizational inertia just long enough to demonstrate their value. By the way, I'm not talking about a process mandating that every idea go through an Innovation Zone. I'm not out to create additional layers of bureaucracy. The Innovation Zone provides an option for people who can't bring ideas into reality on their own, and it will draw people to it because it increases the likelihood of success with an idea.

For example, imagine that you had a great idea and were given the option of bringing it to market on your own or having a savvy team of venture capitalists, businesspeople, and other astute individuals in your camp to help. Which would you choose? The incentive of an Innovation Zone should be a very personal one that drives the submission of new ideas.

However, success at surfacing more ideas only brings you to the start of the innovation process. Getting from ideas to innovations is a process of creation, collection, evaluation, building, funding, and finally implementing ideas. That means that relatively few of the ideas submitted will actually end up in practice. An innovation process that starts with ten thousand ideas ends up with about thirty innovations. This process of distilling ideas is typical and necessary in organizations that set out to extract maximum value from the innovation process. And the numbers, by the way, are not arbitrary. The ratio of 333 ideas for each innovation is a benchmark that I've often used to illustrate just how much we need to both focus on generating ideas as well as filtering them. Even at an organization such as Procter & Gamble only 10 percent of its patents are actually used in its products![4] The rest are warehoused, licensed, or sold to other companies. However, that 90:10 ratio represents the ideas that did make it

*Quantity of ideas alone is not what drives progress.*

through a patent gate. Each of these reflects at least nine ideas that did not ever make it to patent. As illustrated in Figure 2, each stage of the idea-to-value process must narrow the possible field of ideas dramatically to deliver value quickly.

But don't get confused by focusing just on the mouth of the funnel. I've seen far too many people and organizations get wrapped up in the premise that quantity of ideas alone is what drives progress. It's not. Innovation is about the entire process and the discipline needed to get from the top to the bottom of the funnel.

## Innovation Zone Building Blocks

An Innovation Zone also has some key building blocks that are essential for it to exist and survive as ideas make their journey through the process in our funnel. Take away these building blocks and what you're left with will almost certainly undermine any innovation process.

FIGURE 2. **THE PATH FROM INVENTION TO INNOVATION**

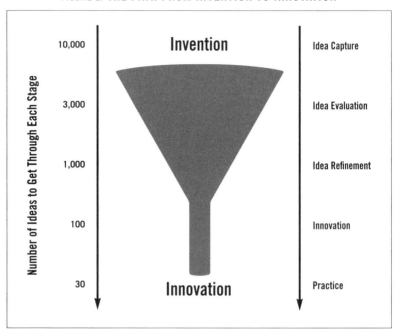

The path from invention to innovation requires both the generation of many new ideas and the ability to filter them quickly and focus on those ideas that have value.

Here is a brief discussion of the importance of each of these building blocks.

**Idea ownership.** Idea ownership is critical to acknowledge and preserve if an organization is to foster a climate and culture where ideas are contributed and not hoarded or hidden for fear of their being co-opted. In organizations where an Innovation Zone thrives, idea owners are recognized and rewarded. In some cases they receive monetary rewards, but more often the value of the new ideas is integrated into employee performance management.

**Idea evaluation.** Ideas that are generated and brought to the table need to be evaluated fairly and transparently so that owners trust the processes by which their ideas will be considered. The organization needs a published set of values, including examples of successful ideas, and a feedback mechanism that critiques ideas.

**Idea championship.** Idea championship differs from ownership in that it defines the way in which an Innovation Zone will bring together a team with the right talent to give the idea the best chance of fair evaluation and success. Idea champions are often respected, neutral, and high-integrity insiders who can facilitate the involvement of the right parties in bringing an idea to fruition.

**Idea storage.** Idea storage is a simple term for capturing ideas that are not immediately applicable to a problem at hand but may be valuable in the future. Too many organizations have no way to preserve ideas if they are not immediately applicable to a customer or market challenge; companies such as 3M make idea storage one of their keys to success.

**Idea valuation.** Lastly, idea valuation is the process of measuring the value of an idea. This is critical but often considered too difficult to do since many ideas may either be only part of an innovation or not directly convertible to a dollar value. For instance, what is the value of a new way to serve a customer if it is only one part of the customer experience? It is possible to measure the overall value of innovation on an organization's business, but measuring an individual idea can be very difficult. The point, however, is to put some sort of metric in place, even if it is qualitative and subjective. Something as simple as public acknowledgment of valuable ideas can be a powerful tool to encourage the right behavior.

Remember, shaping a culture of innovation is as much a part of an Innovation Zone as is anything else you may do to foster innovation. An Innovation Zone ensures that these building blocks exist in an organization and are combined into a single process that constantly generates and filters new ideas.

Keep in mind that the ideas that flow through an Innovation Zone can be incremental or radical. They can be tactical or strategic. As long as they reflect a change that adds some value, they qualify as innovative. If that value is measured and the people who create it are rewarded, innovation can become part of any organization's culture and systems.

## Putting an Innovation Zone in Place

So stop and think about what innovation means to your organization. Do you have an idea-to-value process in place? Do you recognize the building blocks of innovation? For instance, do you measure the value of each innovation, do you track it back to its creator, do you reward the creator based on the value of the innovation, and can you quantify the investment in and the payback from innovation? These are tough questions for most organizations. But they can and must be answered. And more and more companies are rising to the occasion.

For example, Partners HealthCare, which runs a group of very large hospitals in the greater Boston area, has established a group it calls Research Ventures & Licensing (RVL) that is dedicated to identifying, nurturing, investing in, measuring, and tracking all new ideas. A process is in place for assessing ideas in a transparent and open manner, then developing the ideas with the creator to pick a path for commercializing the idea. Finally, any value derived from the idea is put back into the organization, with a specific amount flowing directly back to the inventor. These are all missing links in most organizations that try to go from invention to innovation. By the way, the RVL leader reports directly to the CEO.

The result at Partners has been enormous value creation and the institutionalization of innovation as a core part of the organizational landscape. The introduction of RVL has resulted in a 30 percent year-over-year increase in new inventions, a dozen new start-ups, and $327 million in revenues from the innovation of these ideas.[5] While some of the innovations coming out of Partners through RVL are blockbuster ideas, such as the new drug Enbrel, the vast majority of ideas the RVL commercializes are incremental changes, but still changes that add measurable value. That's an important point—if you can't measure the value of incremental innovations, you end up in the predicament of depending on blockbusters to prove you're innovative. That's a huge mistake that causes your perception, as well as the market's perception, of your organization as an innovator to suffer.

*The last thing you can afford is to let good ideas bleed out of your organization by frustrating and alienating their owners.*

Look, the truth is that innovation in a free market economy is always relative. There are no absolutes; you need only innovate faster than your competitors. But what has changed in today's world is that your biggest and most innovative competitors will come from the place you least expect. As you look to the left they will pass you on the right, with your former best employee behind the wheel.

Ideas flow much more freely than they ever have. The last thing you can afford is to let good ideas, however small, however different, bleed out of your organization by frustrating and alienating their owners. Building and maintaining an Innovation Zone is the way to capture the ideas and keep their owners engaged.

So how do you begin building an Innovation Zone? By looking at how innovation happens on the front lines. Getting into the Innovation Zone begins with looking at how others have made their way in. The zone isn't about dogma; there's plenty of that sort of motherhood and apple pie to go around when people talk about innovation. What matters is the practice and process of innovation, and how to emulate the behaviors, attitudes, and tactics of innovators who have been there, done it, and done it again, and again, and again.

## Innovation Recap

Innovation is intimately tied to uncertainty, and this means that innovation is not something that can be easily predicted. Instead it is necessary to put in place processes by which organizations can quickly mobilize to innovate for unanticipated opportunities and challenges. The foundation of this is the "uncertainty principle," which illustrates how increased volatility, uncertainty, and opportunity create ever-decreasing windows of opportunity to respond. This applies not only to product and service innovation but to business model innovation.

The Five Laws of Innovation define the common characteristics of innovative individuals and organizations:

- Innovation is dangerous.

- Innovators are impervious to rejection.

- Innovation is not invention.

- Innovation is not a solo flight.

- Innovation is *always* a threat to yesterday's success.

All this makes it essential to set up an Innovation Zone, creating a protected space where ideas can be identified, evaluated, nurtured, and developed to create value.

CHAPTER 2

# BUILDING AN INNOVATION PROCESS

*Turn and run if anyone tells you, "I can't teach you how to innovate. You have to be born that way." It's certainly possible to point to people and companies that are exceptional at innovation, but does that mean you aren't innovative? Of course not. Human beings are wired to innovate. If you doubt that, take a look at your kids, grandkids, or nieces or nephews, especially between the ages of six and nine: They are born innovators and they prove beyond any doubt that innovation is fundamental to the human condition. You were born an innovator—we all were—but somewhere along the line you grow up.*

All too often we think of innovation as a moment of inspiration followed by an invention; for example, the moment Edison's lightbulb came to life. The grandeur of those moments tends to eclipse the thousands of times Edison's lightbulbs sputtered and died and the perseverance and processes it took to get to the point of illumination. Innovation is a process, not an event.

In my own dealings with large organizations I've seen time and time again that the companies that get innovation right and sustain it are those that can make innovation systemic and systematic, that think of the process of being innovative rather than the specific product. In other words, innovation is part of what they do every day—

not once a decade when a crisis looms. Marketing programs and periodic spurts of growth will capture the limelight and make it look as though these companies suddenly came upon the best thing since indoor plumbing, when in fact they have been consistently innovating behind the scenes for many years.

*Great innovation is the result of a sustained process of countless repetitions, each of which fine-tunes the innovation to the market's needs.*

Even classic consumer success stories such as the Walkman fall into this category of innovations that give the illusion of invention. Sony was incredibly transparent for many years as it rolled out dozens of models of Walkman technology. Likewise, Google was doing little different in how it searched the Internet; its technical inventions were decades old, which is why Google blindsided incumbents with its business model of selling search as an advertising medium. That was the real Google innovation. Yet, despite their transparency, these companies continue to succeed and innovate. That's because great innovation is the result of a sustained process of countless repetitions, each of which fine-tunes the innovation to the market's needs. These processes are the real engines of innovation, and they are much harder to replicate than any single product.

More to the point, these popular icons of innovation are not inventors in the classic sense. They tend to be second or third movers at best. Apple did not invent MP3s (nor the iPod), and Sony did not invent the transistor radio; for that matter, Microsoft did not invent the Windows-based interface, which had been popularized by Apple years earlier and invented at Xerox PARC earlier still, nor did it invent the Internet browser, which was pioneered by Netscape.

Players heralded as pioneers are more often astute settlers. They may not discover the idea, but when they decide to enter a market their persistence of innovative processes and their ability to combine a new business model with existing inventions reshapes that market and defines it in an entirely new way.

My point is that without a solid and sustained process of innovation many great inventions will never get off the ground. Too many obstacles stand in the way. Besides, the real innovation is almost never the product; it is the way value is created through a new business model that acts like a virus, mutating and transporting itself from host to host faster than any existing antibodies—the very real forces I call the "innovation killers"—can defend against it.

## Avoiding Innovation Killers

The innovation killers are almost always disguised as protectors of the organization, or more appropriately protectors of the past. Few people try to kill innovation outright. Their intentions are always good ones: to minimize risk, to deliver predictability, and to satisfy market and analysts' expectations. The innovation killers always have armies of well-intentioned corporate citizens behind them, ready to defend their turf and keep innovation at bay lest it disrupt the status quo.

I've seen at least ten innovation killers come up in my work with organizations, especially large organizations.

### INNOVATION KILLERS

1. Believing that innovation will just happen
2. Telling everyone to "think outside the box," holding a brainstorming session, then calling it a day
3. Laying the success of innovation solely on the shoulders of your technologists
4. Creating an obstacle course for ideas
5. Viewing "different" and "new" as bad
6. Handing over the good ideas to the Legal and Accounting departments
7. Being very, very afraid of failure
8. Innovating only when you need to
9. Leaving it up to the "innovators"
10. Encouraging everyone to drop any and all ideas into an electronic submission box

### INNOVATION KILLER 1: BELIEVING THAT INNOVATION WILL JUST HAPPEN

The belief that innovation will just happen makes about as much sense as the belief that a garden will sprout in your backyard without any planting, weeding, or watering.

Attention to innovation is a requirement in today's world. Even in industries where the margins are slim—such as manufacturing and sourcing—innovation is a must. Here's the irony: You may feel you cannot afford to take a big risk, but that doesn't mean that somewhere on the globe you won't be challenged. As an example of how vulnerable standing still makes you, only think of the U.S. auto industry, now locked in battle against foreign carmakers. You need to lobby for the importance of innovation, and the dollars and owners to support it.

### INNOVATION KILLER 2: TELLING EVERYONE TO "THINK OUTSIDE THE BOX," HOLDING A BRAINSTORMING SESSION, THEN CALLING IT A DAY

Great ideas are the seeds of innovation; they are not innovation itself. Ideas are not in short supply. Spend an hour in a meeting with a few bright people and you will end up with dozens of new ideas. Then what? Where do those ideas go? Who evaluates them and shepherds them through the next stages?

Ideas are not innovation. Companies that get innovation right have a holistic view of innovation and create a culture to ensure that it flourishes. They build, implement, and communicate a process to support innovation, so that everyone knows how it works and is able to participate. In the end you have to have a formalized process for ensuring that ideas are nurtured.

### INNOVATION KILLER 3: LAYING THE SUCCESS OF INNOVATION SOLELY ON THE SHOULDERS OF YOUR TECHNOLOGISTS

Technology should support innovation, not lead it. This is because innovation is first an issue of corporate culture, concerning things like rewards, inspiration, and motivation.

In any situation, you get two activities—the invention and the innovation, or the actual process of innovating. I draw a hard line between the two, and technology's role comes after invention. IT should be involved with implementing the technology that best supports the innovation process. For example, many companies are turning to vendors that offer idea management technology.

### INNOVATION KILLER 4: CREATING AN OBSTACLE COURSE FOR IDEAS

If you want to guarantee a process that kills the innovative spirit, force people to take time away from their regular jobs to defend their new ideas. Look, I'm not trying to sound like a corporate radical, at least not yet, but bureaucracy and Byzantine processes discourage enthusiasm and participation. Ideas need a safe place to take shape. They have to be protected long enough to be evaluated and documented. Make this process even remotely cumbersome and people will just avoid it, allowing their ideas to languish rather than go to the mat every time they have an idea. You'll eventually adopt the tongue-in-cheek mantra of the military: "The last thing you want to do is volunteer!"

### INNOVATION KILLER 5: VIEWING "DIFFERENT" AND "NEW" AS BAD

The number of very smart people I've heard say "That's just not the way we do it around here!" is the single most incredible aspect of my job. If anything is certain in life it is that every single idea we hold as indisputable will eventually be disputed and trumped by another. Barring the most basic moral truths and human values, which we all share, ideas are meant to be disproved and replaced with newer ideas. Yet the fear of the "new" is always present. So the next time you want to say "That's not the way we do it here," try "We prefer to let someone else do it that way and succeed in figuring it out so that they can take our customers away" instead. Doesn't sound as comforting, does it?

Today's world requires companies to become more like Gillette, which is not afraid to eat its young. Gillette invests enormous amounts of money in developing products to compete with existing ones, for one simple reason: If Gillette doesn't innovate on its products, someone else will.

### INNOVATION KILLER 6: HANDING OVER THE GOOD IDEAS TO THE LEGAL AND ACCOUNTING DEPARTMENTS

Ideas are fragile, easily broken or squashed. On the surface, giving the care of those ideas to Legal or Accounting may make sense, since some of the greatest issues with protecting new ideas are legal and financial.

But those with the most influence over the idea process must be the innovation champions, and that emphasis must come from the top. Create support and ownership for innovation at management's uppermost tiers.

### INNOVATION KILLER 7: BEING VERY, VERY AFRAID OF FAILURE

I've found that failure-tolerant management is the third most important ingredient in creating an innovative culture. Although it's possible to build an iterative process and lessen the cost of a failure, the bottom line is that the market is fickle and you can't predict what will happen.

Here's the scary truth: You will fail sometimes. Like a child learning to ride a bike, you simply cannot move ahead without taking a few knocks. The question is: Are you in the kind of organization that can embrace innovation in spite of that? What doesn't work out is merely a learning experience and therefore fodder for the innovation cycle. Use case studies, research, and other support to show naysayers why learning experiences are a must in today's corporate environment.

## INNOVATION KILLER 8: INNOVATING ONLY WHEN YOU NEED TO

It's tantalizing to innovate on demand. It appears to cost less, focuses on specific issues, and provides a rallying cry when a crisis looms. Besides, it is the way most innovation seems to occur. But this is like trying to stay healthy by waiting for a life-threatening condition to arise before paying attention to your health. A crisis is certainly a motivator, but it is also the most expensive way to innovate, in terms of costs, resources, and image.

Unfortunately, we have become accustomed to crisis-driven innovation over the better part of the past two hundred years, as the industrial model was taking shape in many nations globally. Continuing to approach investment in innovation from the standpoint of zero-based budgeting only serves to drive innovation costs up and to reinforce the lack of ongoing processes that contribute to a culture and business model of continuous innovation.

## INNOVATION KILLER 9: LEAVING IT UP TO THE "INNOVATORS"

Every organization has a handful of people who are considered to be the thought leaders. Sometimes they are the leaders, other times well-tenured individuals, and sometimes people tasked with coming up with big ideas. In all these cases the implication is that only these big thinkers can come up with big ideas. It may be true that these are the brightest minds of the organization, but ideas can and should come from anyone in the organization. Focusing on just the "big" ideas or just the "big" minds is equally dangerous as it creates barriers for incremental innovation and encourages ideas to find an exit elsewhere. This is not to say that you might not need someone to come in and help you understand the process of innovation and jump-start your Innovation Zone, but it has to become *your* Innovation Zone.

## INNOVATION KILLER 10: ENCOURAGING EVERYONE TO DROP ANY AND ALL IDEAS INTO AN ELECTRONIC SUBMISSION BOX

This last one may surprise you. After all, isn't the whole point of innovation and the theme of this book to encourage idea submission? Yes, but with a very important caveat: Every innovation effort submitted must be evaluated, checked for practicality and suitability for the organization. Some of the biggest failures I've seen involve companies whose ambition to solicit ideas far exceeded their capacity to evaluate them. The reality is that when you ask someone to submit an idea you have to acknowledge it with a sincere evaluation, no matter how silly the idea may appear. Organizations make two fatal mistakes here.

First, they put one part-time person at the narrow end of a very large funnel of new ideas. This is a setup for disaster; no one person can keep up with the flow, and it's too easy to shoot down ideas that don't pass some unwritten code of acceptability.

Second, the ideas languish in a nondescript repository with no taxonomy to group them, combine them, and make it possible to mine them. Ideas need to be treated with respect. Whatever systems you put in place must have boundaries for what constitutes an idea submission. For example, what core values or hurdles must it be able to pass? You must have a transparent process for the evaluation. And finally, you need to involve the submitter and communicate the idea's status. I often use the analogy of dropping a child off at day care. Parents who use day care are justifiably concerned and ask the day care provider many questions before they will leave their child. What is the environment children will be in? Will they be cared for and nurtured? Will parents be involved, contacted, counseled if needed? Will children benefit from the experience? All of these are the same sorts of questions that need to be asked of the brainchildren entrusted to an innovation management system.

*Some of the biggest failures I've seen involve companies whose ambition to solicit ideas far exceeded their capacity to evaluate them.*

Overcoming the ten innovation killers can be a daunting challenge for many organizations. The innovation killers are not behaviors that change overnight. They require a sustained and systemic approach. The best way to begin chipping away at them is to put in place a team whose specific responsibility is to nurture innovation throughout the organization by establishing an Innovation Zone where new ideas can take root. It's key that such a team does not own or co-opt new ideas, but instead nurtures and grows them.

## Building an Innovation Capability

It's fine to avoid the innovation killers, but how does an organization build an innovation capability? I've seen six clear success factors.

### SIX INNOVATION SUCCESS FACTORS

- Dedicated function
- Incentives for inventors
- Internal exit
- Metrics
- Integrated information
- Leadership

**Dedicated function.** Successful innovation starts with establishing a dedicated function to institutionalize the process in a fair and transparent manner. This function must have the skills needed to interface with the many constituents of an innovation and commercialization effort or to be able to undertake the task and its associated risks on its own.

**Incentives for inventors.** Inventors must have real incentives to share their ideas with the full confidence that the ideas will be treated fairly and equitably from concept to commercialization. When the ideas are submitted, they must be taken seriously and fairly evaluated, whatever their source or state of completion.

**Internal exit.** The organization must set up an internal exit so that owners of new ideas can share in the value of commercialization. The exit has to be clearly spelled out and must involve an investment of expertise in the areas of commercialization where inventors are necessarily weak—that is, in legal, business, partnering, licensing, and funding functions.

**Metrics.** Metrics must be established so that innovation can be demonstrated to all stakeholders and gauged and critiqued by them.

**Integrated information.** The core competencies of the business must be supported by integrated information systems that allow cross-organizational sharing of information, trends, practices, and customers.

**Leadership.** The organization's leaders must embrace the concept of innovation over the long term.

The following case study illustrates how these success factors interact.

## Case Study: Partners HealthCare

In the health care and medical research sectors, new ideas are critical to building on the rich intellectual property of highly educated researchers, doctors, and caregivers. Partners HealthCare, a Boston-based integrated health system, understands the challenge very well. It has invested in a business unit dedicated to identifying, evaluating, funding, and commercializing ideas within its network of hospitals in the northeastern United States. The nonprofit organization's Research Ventures & Licensing (RVL) group provides a model for any large organization that places a premium on its employees' creativity and the value of innovation.[1]

*The Partners HealthCare Innovation Zone is an environment in which distinct disciplines and otherwise separate health care professionals can collaborate—and are motivated to do so.*

### HOW RVL BRIDGES IDEAS AND INNOVATION

The centerpiece of the Partners HealthCare Innovation Zone is the creation of an environment in which distinct disciplines and otherwise separate health care professionals can collaborate—and are motivated to do so. But collaboration is not just about changing behavior. It requires infrastructure, tools, processes, tactics, and mechanisms that not only support the right behaviors but also introduce new skills and systems that are radically different from those found in most research organizations.

The primary objective of RVL is to become more effective at growing and nurturing new scientific discoveries. The group's secondary objective is to shepherd discoveries through the risky and complex processes of commercialization. Both objectives are equally important, but it is the latter that is the true measure of an innovation culture.

RVL's success in this regard is difficult to dispute. In 2006 RVL succeeded in generating 449 inventions—a 30 percent increase over 2005, as touched on earlier. Of these, nearly half were submitted for patent protection, representing a 20 percent increase for the same period. In addition, RVL formed twelve new start-ups to commercialize inventions and realized a whopping $327 million in license income from its innovations.[2]

While some of RVL's discoveries have been blockbuster-caliber drugs, the vast majority of its commercial discoveries represent incremental innovations across the health care spectrum.

*An Innovation Zone is built to deliver a steady stream of reliable value.*

This is a point that is easy to miss. RVL represents a continuous process for innovation and as such it is defined by a continuous accretion of value, not just a periodic spike in value. The lesson here is a key one. An Innovation Zone is built to deliver a steady stream of reliable value. Occasionally a by-product of that process may be a home run, but that is not the primary mission of an Innovation Zone.

## AN INNOVATION STORY

One of the most common infections acquired in an intensive care unit (ICU) is aspiration pneumonia, a condition in which fluid fills the lungs, creating potentially serious complications. The problem typically occurs when a patient's bed is not tilted at between thirty and forty-five degrees to the horizontal. Conventional tilt-recording devices do not indicate if the bed is at the correct angle. They simply mark off every five degrees of angle, making it time-consuming and confusing to adjust a bed.

An ICU doctor at a Partners HealthCare hospital got his inspiration for a device to quickly rectify the problem when watching a Starbucks barista heat milk for a beverage. He noticed that when the milk was adequately heated the dial indicator on the coffee machine reached the red zone. He designed a device that attaches to a bedside and shows vividly, using green and red color bands, when the bed is at the correct angle.

In many research scenarios, this is as far as such inventions go—one location benefits from it, but no one else picks it up. In this case, however, the idea was presented to RVL. The group called in a supply chain of partners, including lawyers, manufacturers, distributors, and the many other commercial elements needed to bring an idea to market. In effect, RVL became the internal incubator for the idea, and the whole organization benefited from it. Simple ideas can create enormous value if a process is in place to capture and develop them.

## UNDERSTANDING RVL'S INNOVATION PROCESS

RVL's charter is to develop, embed, and institutionalize the mechanisms needed to increase innovation effectiveness. These objectives can end up at odds with one another. The problem is that inventors often view a formal innovation process as a "black box" that takes control away from them. For an inventor to share an idea and allow it to be evaluated, a strong element of trust must be in place. RVL has developed that trust by creating a transparent process for the evaluation of new ideas.

RVL has institutionalized the innovation process, making it explicit. To do so, it has published a set of criteria against which every new idea must be evaluated in order to identify its stage of readiness and to highlight the most appropriate actions for moving the idea, from filing for patent protection to funding and development. While the process is rigorous and somewhat complex, it is designed to make decisions about the visibility of new ideas in an equitable and effective fashion.

*For an inventor to share an idea and allow it to be evaluated, a strong element of trust must be in place.*

The process initially determines if a new idea is ready and suitable for patenting. If so, then the idea is guided toward the appropriate commercial pathway: as a license, a proof-of-principle investment, further R&D, a start-up, or in a co-investment model. According to staff, approximately 50 percent of new ideas make it past the patent gateway.

This is a critical and unique value of RVL—a competency easily lost on a casual observer and difficult to emulate. To succeed with this secondary element of innovation, RVL pulls together a long list of disciplines so it can provide the necessary legal, business, scientific, capital markets, regulatory, and leadership skills needed to follow any of the five paths to commercialization.

A simple way to think about the RVL approach is to imagine all of the organizational groups involved in bringing any new idea to market in your organization. The list would include representatives from each of your functional groups (legal, accounting, marketing, sales, product development, and the rest). Now consider having these same skills in a subgroup of individuals whose responsibility it is to evaluate each new idea and then to determine whether it is ready to be commercialized and, if so, how that should happen.

*RVL has a perpet-ual skunk works in place, constantly churning new ideas and giving them safe harbor—an Innovation Zone.*

In fact, the idea is far from hypothetical. Many organizations have what is typically referred to as a *skunk works,* an incubator for the development of special projects; that was what led to the genesis of IBM's personal computer and of Sun's Java Web language. However, such initiatives are outside mainstream R&D activities. RVL has a per-petual skunk works in place, constantly churning new ideas and giv-ing them safe harbor—an Innovation Zone. If a discovery carries too much risk for its inventor's organization, RVL has the autonomy to absorb a portion of the risk by taking the innovation forward.

One way that risk bearing is being realized at RVL is through a new $35 million fund called the Center for Innovative Ventures (CIV). The CIV's sole purpose is to fund start-ups and NewCos (new companies) formed around ideas in too early a stage for funding through traditional sources. By using this fund to jump-start ideas that may not be ready for other paths to commercialization, RVL can develop such ventures into larger long-term opportunities. In those cases, RVL is relying on its unique blend of domain and venture expertise to seize opportunities that may be difficult for outsiders to appreciate. The CIV also allows RVL to co-invest when a significant new idea *does* attract outside capital.

The last point to make about RVL's innovation management dis-cipline is the impact it has on budgeting for innovation. In most organizations, dollar set-asides for innovation quickly become com-plex political battlegrounds, and secrecy is the norm. Instead, RVL makes the evaluation of new ideas transparent to all parties. This may well be one of the hardest things to do in organizations accustomed to the "black box" style of decision making about innovation.

## NOT JUST ANOTHER INVESTMENT MECHANISM

It's important to keep in mind that RVL is more than just an inside version of an outside investor. While RVL does indeed look at the economic aspects of commercializing innovation, it also considers carefully the way in which innovation candidates align with and support the mission of Partners HealthCare—that is, whether they truly help to improve health care. That is not to say that RVL is a philanthropic or charitable institution either (although Partners HealthCare is). In practice, the unit defines economic hurdles based on the factors that best support Partners' mission but that may otherwise not be attractive to an outside investor.

That last point is key. It speaks to the importance of recognizing the value of internal innovation that may not easily be seen or recognized by outsiders. Nurturing such opportunities internally is a way to jump-start new ideas and bring them to the point where they can meet more aggressive economic hurdles for capital investment in the open market.

RVL also has to act as a risk-balancing mechanism. One of the unit's key insights was the realization that it needed to balance the legal and business views of the innovation process. Over time, too much emphasis on protecting Partners from risk or too much zeal for exploiting potential market opportunities might undercut the value of effective innovation management.

While it would be nice to present a formula by which RVL strikes the right risk–reward balance, it simply cannot be done. Each innovation is unique. The only constants are having the ability to look at innovation from all vantage points in a fair and objective manner. In effect, RVL arbitrates, augments, and aligns the many interests and parties necessary for effective innovation to occur. Whatever industry you're in, that has to be part of the innovation process.

## THE INTERNAL EXIT

The institutionalization of innovation means that Partners' inventors are provided with what RVL calls an "internal exit"—a way to take their ideas to market without leaving the company.

The idea of an internal exit is not new. Many organizations, such as Xerox PARC, Bell Labs, and numerous academic partnerships, have attempted to create similar environments to encourage employees to develop their ideas in-house. The difference at RVL is that the internal group is not the creator or developer of the idea—it is the facilitator. RVL is not a lab or an R&D function in any sense of the term. Instead it is an orchestrator between the idea's creator and the many forces and parties that must participate if the idea is to be put into practice or commercialized. Of course, mutual economic incentives and rewards are the essence of any business partnership. This is no different at RVL, where scientists generally receive 25 percent of royalties for their discoveries. However, recognition can come in many forms, not just monetary.

In an era marked by speed and sheer volume of innovation, the internal exit is a critical mechanism to retain human capital and also to liberate the power of innovative thinking. The real benefit of giving employees internal exits is long term: creating a group of in-house inventors who over time provide myriad valuable new ideas.

*In an era marked by speed and sheer volume of innovation, the internal exit is a critical mechanism to retain human capital and also to liberate the power of innovative thinking.*

This has proven to be the case within the Partners HealthCare system, where several researchers, scientists, and doctors have become nothing less than innovation engines. In turn, these exemplary innovators motivate others in the organization to develop and submit their ideas. The ultimate manifestation of a well-developed innovation program is the appearance of a subset of innovators who repeatedly bring new ideas to the table alongside a larger population that contributes periodically.

Of course, that means that RVL has to continue motivating potential innovators—pushing them beyond their normal day-to-day activities while also making the time to review and respond to subsequent ideas, even if many of the ideas are not practical, either commercially or to advance the organization's mission.

## A LONGITUDINAL VIEW OF TECHNOLOGY

One additional aspect of RVL that could easily go unnoticed is that it is not only a one-stop center of expertise for innovation but also a place of deep domain understanding in health care. Without that understanding RVL would not be able to build the necessary bonds of trust with potential innovators. Nor would it be able to adequately or equitably evaluate the ideas submitted.

RVL also has access to an additional resource: It can tap Partners' information systems to significantly increase its chances for success with new ideas. This is what Partners refers to as the *longitudinal patient record*, a file that cuts across the entire Partners HealthCare network. Each hospital has full access to a patient's data, history, and treatments. This provides a significantly better level of care, but it can also be an invaluable asset for evaluating how certain patients respond to specific treatments.

This approach has the potential to turn medicine on its head. The thinking in medicine has historically been that you start with a hypothesis and then test it on patients. With access to enormous stores of data, the thinking is shifting to the creation of new and unpredictable hypotheses sourced from patient data. In other words, as the patient data is mined and massaged, the data start to suggest paths to new discoveries.

The lesson in what Partners plans to do with longitudinal patient records is not limited to health care. In most every industry, a limiting factor to innovation is the inability to link information about cause and effect across the enterprise. This failure limits organizations' ability to recognize and respond to opportunities as well as challenges.

The core principle at work is one of boosting response times by better integrating the underlying information needed to support the organization's core competency. Partners' core competency is the coordination of quality health care across a network of specialists and providers. The derivative benefit of increased innovation ultimately feeds back into that core competency. Effective innovation processes should always work that way.

## Investing in an Innovation Zone

There is much to be learned from the RVL example that can be applied to innovation in every organization and industry. The question is not whether or not to innovate, but rather at what cost. The costs are tallied not only in dollars invested to generate new ideas but also in the loss of good ideas to external exits, competitors, start-ups, and organizational barriers.

Innovation is always a risky proposition. Untested ideas can easily disrupt the status quo and increase costs without a known return. Many organizations continue to stumble along with innovation through serendipity and brute force. Even in industries touted for their ability to innovate, such as pharmaceuticals, the process involves enormous investment in trial and error.

*The costs of innovation are tallied not only in dollars invested to generate new ideas but also in the loss of good ideas to external exits, competitors, start-ups, and organizational barriers.*

Organizations are littered with great ideas that wither and die before they ever get close to the market. The tools needed to get these ideas across the divide from invention to innovation are the responsibility of leadership. These tools require cross-industry investments that can rarely be justified within discrete profit-driven business units. They require ownership and processes that are strategic in terms of investment and return. They require independence in the evaluation of new ideas and in nurturing them to fruition.

In the case of RVL at Partners, the investment in innovation takes the form of a specific business unit, which is ultimately funded through its own success. But getting the initial investment to start this sort of a process has stalled many an innovation effort, in large part because of the difficulty of predicting how any innovation will evolve and where and how the investment will pay off.

There has never been a large company that did not one day wake up to find itself displaced in some way by a more agile competitor. The cost of being in this position and trying to recover from it is infinitely higher than the cost of developing new ideas.

One of the things that's especially interesting about the life cycle of innovation is the way in which it often departs from its anticipated trajectory and evolves into an entirely new value proposition. This is the case even for some of the most radical innovations. Shopping over cable TV, for example, was thought of as nothing more than a curiosity when it was first broadcast by the Home Shopping Network (originally the Home Shopping Club—HSC) in 1981. Yet the quirky format and community involvement on the part of regular shoppers who were integrated into the program by phone to attest to their satisfaction has been a long-term success, continuing even in the age of Internet shopping. Originally the idea behind HSC was to simply provide a convenient way to sell overstocked products by reaching a vast audience. But the business model quickly changed to a means for connecting a huge community in the same way shopping malls had decades earlier. Shopping through a catalog certainly didn't offer that option. And even online shopping does not offer the real-time experience of listening to other shoppers and sharing your own views in real time, while watching supplies of the item being sold quickly dwindle as others purchase it. It was like going to a store and being drawn to a line of shoppers. These were essential elements in home shopping but barely part of the original model.

Great organizations invest in the process of innovation above and beyond any particular innovation.

The fact is that both education and experiencing how things have been done work against us when it comes to predicting the future potential of a new idea. Each acts as a funnel narrowing our field of vision so tightly that eventually we only see what's already behind us. Gaining visibility requires us to look beyond what's possible to what's impossible. We consistently underestimate the magnitude of new discoveries, since the temptation is always to focus on the obstacles. To paraphrase Edison, "We can all find ten thousand reasons why a new idea won't work."

*Both education and experiencing how things have been done work against us when it comes to predicting the future potential of a new idea.*

If it's impossible to predict the full benefit of innovation, how do we justify investing in it? you may well ask. Great question. The answer is, you don't. There is no "it" to invest in.

Great organizations invest in the process of innovation above and beyond any particular innovation. In the case of HSN, the "it" wasn't selling stuff on TV; there was nothing new there. The "it" was the community experience, and the challenge was to create an event facilitated by trained on-air talent and backed up with the ability to quickly integrate listeners into the collection of active participants.

Innovation requires an open organizational mind that is not so attached to a product that it builds defenses to block out new ideas. This sort of openness begins with the example and commitment of leadership.

## Innovation Recap

Innovation needs to be a system: a process of being innovative rather than a specific *product*. While products have dominated our notion of innovation, enduring value is created through a new business model that is able to recombine existing ideas and inventions to create new value.

Ten innovation killers stand in the way of innovation in most organizations:

- Believing that innovation will just happen
- Telling everyone to "think outside the box," holding a brain-storming session, then calling it a day
- Laying the success of innovation solely on the shoulders of your technologists
- Creating an obstacle course for ideas
- Viewing "different" and "new" as bad
- Handing over the good ideas to the Legal and Accounting departments
- Being very, very afraid of failure
- Innovating only when you need to
- Leaving it up to the "innovators"
- Encouraging everyone to drop any and all ideas into an electronic submission box

On the other side, six success factors make it more likely that an organization will build a workable innovation process:

- Dedicated function
- Incentives for inventors
- Internal exit
- Metrics
- Integrated information
- Leadership

CHAPTER **3**

# LEADING INNOVATION

*In research I conducted just after the World Trade Center attack on 9/11 I posed the question, "What factor creates the highest level of certainty in your organization's ability to deal with uncertainty?" The prevalent answer to that question— by a wide margin—was "leadership." When an organization encounters a crisis requiring it to build for the unknown, the role of leadership takes on a critical responsibility to counterbalance the intuitive tendency to become even more risk averse by hunkering down and adopting a bunker mentality.*

The single most consistent element of those organizations that sustain innovation is found in one word, *leadership*. While innovation is deeply rooted in cultural behaviors across an organization, the license and the mandate to value innovation always starts with leadership, and specifically at the highest levels with the CEO. But paying lip service to the idea of innovation is not enough. I've seen many a value statement that includes a reference to innovation but lacks follow-up.

Leaders who expect their organization to achieve high levels of sustained innovation have to overcome organizational inertia and focus on four distinct objectives that foster innovation.

First, they have to separate the core competencies of the organization from its core business model. Doing this allows an organization to innovate within its core business and also to build new business models. These two are competing objectives that vie for the same resources. Balancing the two and establishing a threshold of investment outside the core business is the responsibility of the leader.

Second, leaders must establish a culture of innovation that includes the behaviors and attitudes needed to sustain innovation. This cuts much deeper than simply adding innovation to a set of organizational values. Culture needs constant reinforcement and programs that build a shared vision across the organization.

Third, leaders must counterbalance the entrenchment that often accompanies success. As organizations prosper they develop a reservoir of faith in the behaviors, attitudes, and processes that allowed them to succeed in the first place. While this reinforces success it also reinforces a natural inclination to stay the course, which can cause a rigid mind-set that interferes with accepting and exploring new ideas and recognizing new trends.

Fourth, leaders must create an organizational structure that fosters innovation throughout the organization in an unimpeded manner, while also providing operational efficiency. Again these are two objectives that frequently conflict, requiring leadership to develop a balance between them.

### THE FOUR OBJECTIVES LEADERS MUST FOCUS ON TO INCREASE INNOVATION

- Separating core competencies from the core business model
- Building and reinforcing a culture of innovation
- Counterbalancing entrenchment in past success
- Creating an organizational structure that facilitates innovation

## Leading to the Core

These are the three questions I consistently ask any leader concerned with creating higher levels of innovation:

- What is your organization's core competency?

- What is your organization's core business model?

- How are you innovating in both?

Organizations increasingly recognize a mandate to focus on what is core and to shed the rest so as to truly differentiate themselves and the value they bring to the market. Yet this is a delicate balance. If a core competency is defined too narrowly, it can be restrictive and make it almost impossible to spot new trends. In addition, if core competencies are confused with the core business model, an organization will quickly lose the ability to innovate.

A *core competency* is an ability to deliver value based on deeply rooted capabilities, values, and culture. These almost always trace back to the founding of an organization and its original mission. Core competencies don't change much unless the organization is dismantled, acquired or merged, or thrust into a severe crisis. *A core business model* is the way you extract value, at any given time, from your core competencies. Core business models can change.

If this distinction seems obscure, try a simple thought experiment. What is your organization's core competency? Answer that in five words or less before you read on.

If you answered with a product, a service, or even a business model, then you need to rethink the question. Most of us think of core competency as a product or a service, but these are fleeting and far too narrow to allow sustained innovation. It's also the reason so many companies get stuck in an outdated market. Core competency cuts much deeper and lasts much longer than any single product, service, or business model. It forms the basis for innovation over time and across products. A core competency is reflected in the core business model of an organization but it does not limit the way an organization innovates its business model.

*Most of us think of core competency as a product or a service, but these are fleeting and far too narrow to allow sustained innovation.*

That's why one of the first tasks of leadership, when it comes to innovation, is to make it a priority to focus on core competency and advertise it broadly. This acts as a compass setting for innovation.

This need not be especially elaborate or precise. One of the best expressions of core competency I ever heard was from Andy Grove, when he was CEO of Intel, who said that Intel's core competency was "the guts of modern computing." How much simpler can you get? But notice that this definition does not talk about silicon wafers, microcircuits, or transistors, nor does it limit how value is created. The guts of a computer might just as well be based on some biological mechanism, and the business model might involve any number of possibilities. This balance between definition and direction sets an imaginary boundary around what the scope of innovation is for an organization in a way that allows for extension beyond the current products and services, and for infinite flexibility around the business model.

This essential point is often lost in many discussions of core competency. In my experience understanding and articulating core competency is only possible with strong, committed leadership that has been at the helm for a reasonable period of time. Admittedly, the liability in this is that the competency sometimes becomes synonymous with the leader—think of Jack Welch and GE or Bill Gates and Microsoft. When leadership changes, an organization can enter a period of soul-searching. However, if the leader has sufficiently articulated the organization's core competency and has been able to demonstrate sustained innovation, the likelihood is that this disruption will be eclipsed by the culture that has been created—as is the case with both GE and Microsoft.

## Leading from the Core

The other aspect of core competency that seems to be uncannily consistent is that organizations that understand their core competency also excel at continuous innovation. They innovate from the foundation of a core competency that remains intact, which lends continuity to innovation as a process rather than a single event.

I've seen time and time again that the innovative companies are the ones that make innovation systemic by focusing on their core competency and looking for ways to use it to meet the changing needs of the market, economic, and social context. More important, this effort is part of what they do every day, not once a decade. Marketing programs and periodic spurts of growth will capture the limelight and make it look as though these companies suddenly came upon a startling innovation out of the blue, when in fact they have been doing what every core competency organization does best, innovating relentlessly behind the scenes.

Leaders need to foster tolerance on the part of their investors in the inherent risk of this sort of continuous innovation and its alignment with the organization's core.

But what if an organization begins to struggle with its market position? Is it time to redefine the core competency? Rarely. In these cases leadership's role is instead to challenge the core business model of the organization. In tumultuous times, any organization requires leadership with a long-term dedication to redeveloping the organization's core competency by limiting distractions that may have obscured the core.

*The innovative companies are the ones that make innovation systemic by focusing on their core competency.*

The companies that sustain growth and margin best are the companies that focus on innovations that build on their core competency by innovating their business model. IBM, for example, prospered by shedding noncore businesses, such as its PC unit, which did not build on the organization's core competency of integrated service and solutions. At the same time, IBM built the scale of its global services division, which reflected a new business model.

## Quick Case: IBM

As CEO of IBM, Lou Gerstner took on one of the most visible and largest examples of an organization struggling to find its core. When Gerstner joined IBM in 1993 the company had been rocked by both the advent of the PC and the rise of client server computing. Losses topped $8 billion, and the idea of dismantling IBM into separate businesses was being discussed seriously. Given all this, Gerstner's famous quip—"The last thing IBM needs right now is a vision"—seems to fly in the face of the need for core competency and innovation. But it speaks to what happens to an organization that can't find its core competency.

IBM had become an incredibly distracted company. Gerstner has said that one of the best lessons to take away from the IBM turnaround was "lack of focus is the most common cause of mediocrity." The challenge for Gerstner was to reestablish core competency while redefining the core business model. So what was, and still is, IBM's core competency? Simply put, the ability to integrate solutions that otherwise require myriad pieces. Gerstner refocused IBM on that core competency and created an organization that could build a new business model of services and integration on top of that core. The result was nothing less than the rebirth of IBM. The proof was that when the next revolution, the Internet, came along, IBM was well positioned to step in and build on its core as *the* e-business vendor.

## Leading Outside the Core

Although building on an organization's core competency by creating new business models is key, it's often resisted because it threatens the current business model. However, fear of this disruption can lead people to focus narrowly on the current business model and ignore the emergence of new ways to create value. Leadership in this case is essential to balancing the current model with what might be perceived as an outside threat.

But without leadership willing to build a case for the value that will offset the disruption, discomfort, and distraction it may cause, new business models are unlikely to be tolerated for long by employees and outside stakeholders.

*Many organizations make the mistake of approaching innovation as being so closely linked to the current business model that they lose their peripheral vision.*

The reality is that many organizations make the mistake of approaching innovation as being so closely linked to the current business model that they lose their peripheral vision. Challenging the current business model makes it possible to spot trends and behaviors in the market that may open up entirely new opportunities. In some cases this may not even be something that the organization pursues directly but rather an opportunity to partner or spin off ideas—sometimes even with competitors. For instance, Procter & Gamble has done precisely this by partnering with longtime rival Clorox to develop Clorox's Press 'n Seal and Glad Forceflex trash bags. This taps into that 90 percent of patents, as noted earlier, that P&G files but never uses for internal P&G products. Another example is DuPont. One of DuPont's core competencies is safety, which goes back to its origins as a gunpowder manufacturer. Realizing this, the company created a Safety Resources business that works with other companies to help them improve their safety record. DuPont then earns a portion of the savings delivered to the client.

These sorts of approaches to commercializing core competency through new business models typically represent business streams worth hundreds of millions of dollars to large companies. But are they core? Only if leadership encourages creative thinking at the periphery, and in some cases well outside the current core business model, to translate the company's core competencies into new value.

This is where leadership needs to provide license to an organization to look far enough beyond the current business models to keep that door to the future open. Without this visible commitment on the part of leadership, rewards, incentives, and career opportunities will all reinforce a short-term focus.

By the way, don't confuse the sort of investment in innovation I'm describing here with investment in R&D. Having an R&D function is critical, but it does not provide what I've been discussing. R&D is a focused and narrow segment of innovation, product specific and rarely resulting in new business models. Typically, it is objective driven, working on solutions to known problems. It's also measured strictly on the commercial value of its output. Many innovations never extend beyond the four walls of an organization. These are innovations that apply to processes, internal services, and support functions, but they can be just as important as any product. In addition, even many product-specific innovations may originate in areas well outside the classic R&D setting.

## Quick Case: Oracle

From its origins Oracle has been in the very lucrative business of selling software licenses. These represent predictable, recurring revenue streams for Oracle generated by both the steep up-front prices and the ongoing maintenance contracts customers sign. However, the trend toward what is called utility or on-demand computing is threatening this business model by promising to deliver software that can be rented or paid for by the dose as needed. The on-demand business model could easily be seen as a threat to the existing license model of software sales. Not at Oracle.

Larry Ellison, Oracle's chairman and CEO, has pursued on-demand on several fronts, investing in third-party providers and building a separate unit within Oracle to develop on-demand solutions for Oracle's applications. The purpose at Oracle, as it is in any case where a company needs to place bets outside its existing business model, is to expand the notion of how a core competency can be translated into a new core business.

## Leading to an Innovation Culture

Once you've established your core competency and the balance needed to explore the business models you can use to create value from the core, you then need to ask if the culture of the organization will support innovation.

It's become fashionable to talk about a culture of innovation. It's much harder to create one. In the vast majority of cases I've seen, an innovation culture is something that has been programmed into the early DNA of an organization by its founder. These cultures run deep and represent a fundamental value system, as is the case at 3M. But what if your company is not fortunate enough to have an existing culture of innovation? Leadership can create and sustain a culture of innovation, but it requires certain elements.

### FIVE ELEMENTS OF A CULTURE OF INNOVATION

- Visibly committed leadership
- Defined area of responsibility
- Rewards
- Customer involvement
- Mentoring and training

### VISIBLY COMMITTED LEADERSHIP

First, leadership has to be visibly committed to making innovation a priority. As I've already said, this goes beyond including it in a corporate statement of values. Innovation has to rise to the top of the stack of priorities—the key to increasing profitability, customer satisfaction, and other key metrics for the business. The requirements are similar to those of the quality movement of the 1980s, which swept through industry. For quality to become part of the organization's culture it had to become something that was critical to success and therefore measured diligently. Executives were held to standards that could be objectively determined.

While that might appear to be harder to do in the case of innovation, metrics such as innovation velocity, described in chapter 7, can be used to determine changes in an organization's ability to create tangible value from innovation.

## DEFINED AREA OF RESPONSIBILITY

Second, your Innovation Zone has to become a defined area of responsibility within the organization. This means at least one person is named leader or champion of your Innovation Zone. This is not the person who comes up with ideas but the person who manages the process of evaluating new ideas, facilitating their progress through the organization, and coordinating the resources needed to bring an idea to practice. Clearly one person may not be able to do all of that in even a moderately large organization, but you need one point of accountability. Don't expect an Innovation Zone to work without that.

## REWARDS

Third, make sure your reward system recognizes the submission of new ideas and the value that results from ideas that make it through the Innovation Zone to practice or commercialization. This recognition can take many forms, from monetary rewards to a simple acknowledgment. Don't immediately assume that rewards always have to involve cash, and don't underestimate the value of recognition. Organizations such as Intel and Accenture have adopted programs that designate a small number of very innovative individuals as "Fellows." Attaining this title is a prestigious and envied achievement, never bestowed without significant contribution. However, its value goes beyond the benefits that accrue to the Fellow; perhaps more important, it makes a statement about how the organization values innovators and the behaviors they espouse. It is also a clear beacon to those in the organization who aspire to achieve similar recognition. Other organizations take a more directly financial approach, such as Partners HealthCare, discussed earlier, which returns 25 percent of all profits to the originator of the idea. Whatever approach you take, be sure to be consistent, transparent, and sincere in recognizing contribution to innovation.

## CUSTOMER INVOLVEMENT

Fourth, a culture of innovation cannot be sustained for long without direct and frequent involvement of customers in assessing your organization's ability to create value through innovation. I've worked with far too many companies that spend a great deal of time and investment in understanding their perception of their innovation capability, measure innovation internally, and try to promote it within their company but would never think to go directly to the customer and ask, "Are we being innovative and, if so, does it add value for you?" I honestly believe many companies don't want to hear the answer, for fear that it might not support their perceptions or hopes on the topic. I recall one organization that did perform a survey of its customers, asking them to rate its ability to innovate. The company provided to its customers services that were a fairly common commodity. It prided itself on the ability to differentiate itself through exceptional service and the ability to provide novel solutions using deep industry knowledge. However, the survey responses came back with a rather dismal innovation rating. Do you want to guess the response to these results? The people responsible for delivering the service were outraged. "We innovate every day that we work for that client!" was one of the indignant responses I remember.

*To assess your innovation capability, go directly to the customer and ask, "Are we being innovative and, if so, does it add value for you?"*

No doubt the consultants did indeed feel they were innovating. But when I asked them if they documented any of these innovations, the response was (predictably), "We're too busy to do that. We need to keep ourselves focused on doing the work."

What about periodically meeting with the customer to talk about recent innovations and to ask about ways in which new ideas could be incorporated into the services delivered? "The contract doesn't measure us on innovation. We are measured on how well we execute and deliver what the contract requires of us."

The client agreed that the company's service delivery was outstanding, yet what they were looking for was a way that the consultants could deliver more by going beyond what was spelled out in the contract and delivering genuine innovation. However, when I asked the client's representatives if they had taken the lead on asking specifically about ways to innovate, offering incentives for innovation, or periodically sitting down with the consultants to ask about innovation, the response was again predictable. "It's not part of our contract, but we just expect that it will get done. After all, the consultants are the ones in the trenches. They should know if there is room for innovation."

I've seen the same in dozens of cases where innovation is simply expected but never measured, communicated, or even addressed directly as a deliverable. Are we so afraid of the word *innovation* that we can't bring ourselves to use it in defining criteria for its measurement?

The only way to resolve this sort of situation is to tackle it head-on. You have to invoke innovation by name with your customers. You need to put in place agreed-upon ways for you and your customers to measure, document, and value innovation. No matter what industry, whether it is business-to-business or business-to-consumer, the same applies. There is no escaping it—the most innovative companies are the ones recognized by their customers as the most innovative.

## MENTORING AND TRAINING

Lastly, no culture can sustain itself intact without mentorship and training of new members of its community. Organizations need to create a coordinated plan for teaching innovation to their employees and partners. Without a common vocabulary, methods, tools, and metrics, innovation rings hollow. A culture of innovation requires maintenance. You need to revisit it frequently to understand how it is working and where it may need to be refined. You need to teach new employees the best practices and shining examples of innovation in your organization and your industry. Innovation is something that is best learned through examples and cases where it has already been done. This may mean a process of internal or external formal education on innovation for the organization's leadership team. It may involve periodic in-house sessions where employees are trained on innovation methods and tools or even formal broadcasting of innovations that have had a business impact. In short, if you do not make innovation part of the ongoing conversation within the organization, people will find it far too easy to ignore its importance and the role it plays.

*A culture of innovation requires maintenance.*

Even with all this support, an innovation culture cannot be created overnight. In every case described in this book, and in the many more I've witnessed firsthand, it has been a long-term process of care and feeding. I'm reluctant to put an exact time frame on it, but I will tell you that it takes as long to create a culture of innovation as it does to demonstrate success through its application. The good news is that I can also tell you from experience that once such a culture is established, nothing short of a direct nuclear hit can dislodge it. That's because people become fervent proponents of the value innovation has to them individually and to their organization. There is something incredibly empowering and satisfying about being part of a team that can build the future. Few things offer as much feeling of control over one's destiny as the ability to repeatedly innovate out of the present. People who absorb an innovation culture are changed, making it exceedingly difficult for them to ever work someplace where a culture of innovation is not valued. That's not always a good thing for them, since more organizations are still struggling with this than not. But it clearly gives them a benchmark that they will take wherever they go in order to build innovation into the organization they become part of.

But even in those cases where leaders are able to foster a culture of innovation, other obstacles and challenges to innovation still apply, especially in successful organizations.

## Leading to Counterbalance Entrenchment

One of the most treacherous obstacles for any successful organization is what I refer to as the *incumbent syndrome.* Once an industry is well established, an attitude develops that creates the illusion of "*this* is the way we do it." The degree to which organizations can create tunnel vision in these cases is impossible to overestimate. As noted, incumbents typically ignore and dismiss new opportunities for innovation because they feel unable to tolerate failure, reluctant to take resources away from existing revenue-generating activities, and resistant to the threat new ideas may pose to existing investment in current approaches.

*Incumbents build enormous warehouses of knowledge and rationalization to predict their market's behaviors. Inevitably, however, this translates into momentum that reduces their flexibility to change and tolerance of failure.*

Incumbents build enormous warehouses of knowledge and rationalization to predict their market's behaviors. Inevitably, however, this translates into momentum that reduces their flexibility to change and tolerance of failure. This momentum is a completely understandable and natural result, given the tremendous investment incumbents make in the technology, skills, infrastructure, partnerships, suppliers, marketing, and myriad other components of any innovation, whether it be product, process, or service. But as flexibility is reduced, incumbents end up putting breakthrough innovation on life support. They find themselves creating an attachment to their old innovation and forming a very specific model around how it behaves. In many cases they may see the trajectory of the market going in a different direction but are helpless to follow it. The momentum of every innovation ultimately gains enough velocity to prevent establishment of a new trajectory. This is when incumbents become a nearly immovable force of nature. Which is why I bring this point up in a chapter about leadership. The only way I've ever seen to counteract this momentum is through incredibly strong leadership.

Eventually, what was once an innovation ends up in a final state of investment during which complexity increases dramatically relative to other alternatives. It would make sense that at this point a simpler or more effective innovation better suited to the current market would be preferred and have an easy time overtaking the older innovation. However, that is not an easy process. By the time an innovation passes this point and turns into a liability, its switching costs have also climbed, leaving far less flexibility in swapping one process for another. This is the primary reason why so many innovations end up being used long after they have outlived their value and utility. Sometimes switching costs are the actual replacement of physical plants, machinery, or products. In other cases they may simply involve new skills or retraining. The result is the sort of relationship between flexibility, complexity, and value illustrated in Figure 3.

An innovation apex is one of the greatest threats to innovation in an established industry. The key to spotting an innovation apex is to look for the catalysts that represent ways in which the current model might be radically disrupted by forces that did not exist when it was created.

Sony's pocket-sized radio was such a disruption; its success was driven by numerous developments that altered the fundamental purpose and reach of radio, including the social concern of citizens who wanted to be able to listen to emergency broadcasts and instructions in case of nuclear holocaust, the miniaturization of electronics, advances in plastics, the advent of the transistor, and an exploding music industry. Likewise, when the minivan hit the market, similar shifts were occurring in manufacturing. Asian competition was driving the demand for smaller cars and demanding new ideas from U.S.

FIGURE 3. **FLEXIBILITY, COMPLEXITY, AND VALUE**

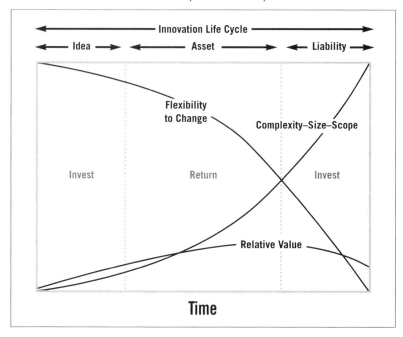

As an innovation matures and its complexity, size, and scope increase, so does the financial and intellectual investment in it. This adds value and increases knowledge but also reduces the flexibility to change the innovation.

automakers; rising real estate costs were driving the flight to more remote suburbs, and the baby boomers, who placed a premium on the convenience of the minivan, and who, by the way, had grown up with the original minivan, the Volkswagen bus, were raising families. In both cases anything less than all of these factors would have been insufficient to ensure their success.

By the way, if you think this last section does not apply to you, don't kid yourself—we all end up being incumbents at some point.

## Leading to a Structure for Innovation

Ultimately innovation will succeed only to the degree to which leadership can integrate innovation into the organization's structure. But this is the greatest challenge of all for leaders of larger organizations. While more distributed and less hierarchical structures tend to work best for innovation in smaller organizations, this sort of free-form structure, which fuels innovation, is exceedingly difficult to preserve as an organization grows.

While the autonomy of a distributed organization can allow individuals to justify and bring to market new ideas without layers of corporate filters, a distributed organization can also be a hindrance to good communication and the sharing of knowledge needed to innovate.

## CENTRALIZED AND DECENTRALIZED ORGANIZATIONS

The fact is that even in the heyday of hierarchical bureaucracy many managers, such as Alfred Sloan, the successful CEO of General Motors from 1923 to 1946, were keenly aware of the virtues of decentralization and autonomy. In Sloan's *My Years with General Motors,* he advocated a hybrid management style of "decentralization with coordinated control." Sloan's description of this model has not lost its relevance against today's backdrop of uncertainty: "From decentralization we get initiative, responsibility, development of personnel, decisions close to the facts, flexibility—in short, all the qualities necessary for an organization to adapt to new conditions."[1]

Sloan's words sound uncannily familiar in the context of innovation. His management model represented some of the first efforts to empower key managers and to recognize their need for some measure of autonomy to react quickly to changing market conditions.

But the paradoxical concepts of decentralization and coordination were not and still are not easy to apply or sustain. As with many companies since, the balance at General Motors shifted more toward coordination and bureaucratic control. It's a natural progression for any organization as it grows and attempts to maintain alignment. It's also the reason that investment in innovation is so desperately needed as a counterbalance to the bureaucracy that works against innovation.

For example, looking back at the inability of the U.S. automotive industry to innovate during the latter part of the twentieth century, it is clearly this ingrained culture of control that accounts for GM, Ford, and Chrysler's painfully slow reaction to changing consumer tastes and strong competition from foreign automobile manufacturers, especially during the late 1970s. Foreign manufacturers were much quicker than their U.S. counterparts to respond to the new consumer demand for smaller and more fuel-efficient vehicles, which resulted from the unforeseen oil crisis in the Middle East. Consequently, as it entered the 1980s, GM saw its sales and profits drop sharply, leading to cutbacks in production and widespread layoffs. At the time, GM did not have an organizational structure that enhanced its customer feedback mechanisms or promoted flexibility and adaptability, effectively creating an organization that barricaded itself from competition and the market. Ultimately this laid the foundation for the development of OnStar, which may be one of the most significant innovations in the automobile industry (see chapter 6).

In an effort to mitigate the ill effects of the typical bureaucracy and maintain the agility needed for innovation to thrive, GM and a host of other corporate behemoths in the same boat developed new, more horizontal organizational formats during the 1970s and 1980s.

Yet, many companies' biggest fear about a decentralized organization was the loss of coordination and the dilution of the organization's coherence and unity of purpose. Would decentralization lead to chaos and confusion among employees? How would employees in a decentralized company identify who is responsible and accountable?

## MATRIX ORGANIZATIONS

The shift to matrix organizations that emphasize decentralization and more localized control was indeed a step in the right direction in the attempt to foster a culture of innovation. The flattened structure promoted local autonomy, which should improve the ability to innovate by creating responsiveness and expediting important decisions, at least relative to a multilayered hierarchy. But matrix controls can still be stifling and intrusive. They also push performance measurement down to a more granular level, which leaves even less discretionary budget for innovation.

Two decades of experimenting with the matrix organization created a long line of failures across many industries, most notably in high-tech, where companies such as HP, IBM, and AT&T all suffered from the toll of endless meetings intended to coordinate the complexity and chaos of a matrix. As a consequence, the ability to innovate and respond creatively to environmental pressures was seriously compromised. Even Sony ran into this problem; many believe that the ultimate downfall of Sony in the MP3 war was caused by its inability to coordinate resources quickly and effectively across its silos to respond as fast as Apple.

The most successful matrix organizations are driven by small teams that tackle projects expeditiously. These teams form the basic "unit of innovation" in all organizations, no matter what their size. The key is to develop the team approach with the right combination of technology and culture and make teams truly a part of the corporate fabric. Ironically, however, even the best and biggest matrix organizations seem to inspire and reward circum-navigating the bureaucracy. In other words, those who advance fastest in these organizations are also those who ignore the limitations of the matrix and simply rally the resources needed to get the job done. This does result in innovation, but it falls far short of building an organization's potential for innovation.

*Be very careful not to fall into the trap of believing that bureaucracy is good because it creates an obstacle course.*

I recall a multibillion-dollar global organization I worked with that had a fascinating chemistry: a well-defined executive hierarchy combined with the intricacies of matrix management. The two cultures interacted like colliding weather fronts. The net result was that those employees who were able to take a good idea and grow it into a new business successfully had to exercise a fair amount of political savvy and on occasion be outright devious in their efforts. If they succeeded, they were lauded and promoted very visibly. If they failed, they were soon cast out.

You may look at that and say, "Well, that's as it should be; only the strong should survive!" There is truth in that, but what this sort of attitude also creates is a culture of fear among many employees who may have brilliant ideas but are highly risk averse and need a job more than they need accolades. Be very careful not to fall into the trap of believing that bureaucracy is good because it creates an obstacle course. Unfortunately, in my experience these obstacles are not differentiators of good ideas from bad ones; they simply separate the bullheaded idea proponents from the less bullheaded. The best ideas will not always be the ones with the most fervent supporters.

## VIRTUAL ORGANIZATIONS

The most recent shift in organizational structure is the move to more virtualized organizations through the use of the Internet. However, keep in mind that networks alone do not define an organization's strategy or what it should be responding to. They merely give it the opportunity to respond faster. Rather than cast organizations as virtual or not virtual, I prefer to think in terms of *virtual relationships* in selected areas, which free the organization to innovate based on its core competencies. This focus on an organization's core through the use of outsourced relationships for noncore functions will often peel away layers of bureaucracy as well as risk. If you focus on what you know and do best, your confidence and latitude in innovating only increases.

The incorrect assumption is that a virtual organization can innovate by managing constantly changing, often unknown resources. I have not seen this done on a broad basis across the many functions of an organization and have serious concerns about its effect on responsiveness.

For certain key innovations, the reliance on the virtual approach could be a fatal mistake. For example, Henry Chesbrough, who popularized the term *open innovation,* differentiates between what he calls autonomous and systemic innovations. "Autonomous innovations can be developed independently from other innovations, while the benefits of systemic innovations can be realized only in conjunction with related, complementary innovations."[2] The benefits of systemic innovations are that they tend to radically alter, and advance, entire industries. Autonomous innovations are much more incremental in their effect.

*But what if entropy is necessary for innovation to thrive?*

Virtual organizations create greater opportunity for developing autonomous innovations. But for systemic innovations the virtual paradigm is probably the wrong choice. It requires a tremendous amount of knowledge to develop and commercialize systemic innovations. This knowledge comes from supplier and customer feedback, employee experiences, research and development, and so forth. The more complex and systemic these innovations tend to be, the more likely they will depend heavily on the ability to mobilize around new ideas. This is difficult to accomplish across a widespread organization.

So what organizational structure is best for innovation?

## LOOSELY COUPLED ORGANIZATIONS

Every form of structure is put in place to counter the entropy that slowly dismantles organizations as they grow. But what if entropy is necessary for innovation to thrive? Perhaps it is only by partially dismantling the organization through periodic interruptions in the market and business that we can continually build it back up again in a form appropriate for new market, economic, and cultural challenges. While it's not possible to disrupt an organization without creating a serious lack of alignment, it is possible to create a mechanism to identify individual ideas that may be disruptive, to nurture those ideas by incubating them as they develop, and then provide an "internal exit," as described with Partners HealthCare's RVL earlier, that enables the idea to survive long enough to build a new critical mass of success around it.

I call this a "loosely coupled" organization because new ideas can exist in local workgroups or smaller businesses that have some level of autonomy and latitude in how they develop innovations. These subgroups can also incubate innovations while they take shape. This ability to handle interruption in the normal course of business is the essential benefit to having an Innovation Zone. It creates a protected space that allows ideas to mature without dismantling the entire organization. Imagine, for instance, telling GM or any automobile manufacturer in the 1980s or '90s that it would someday be out of the manufacturing business and instead making its profits as a relationship manager (for that matter, try telling some of these companies the same today). You would be laughed out of the boardroom and escorted by Security out the front door. Yet this is exactly the kind of sea change that OnStar is creating.

This sort of approach does not create an organizational adhocracy, as Warren Bennis has called it, but it does create a sieve able to capture ideas that might not otherwise survive. These captured ideas are vetted and then loosely coupled with the organization until they can develop. The model is not atypical in large service organizations that operate as partnerships where local groups make investments in innovation for local purposes that can later grow into enterprise-wide processes, services, or products.

Keep in mind, however, that in a loosely coupled organization you still need to create the mechanisms by which new ideas can be funded. This will require either a centralized Innovation Zone function as in RVL, a means of measuring performance based on innovation contributions from the local groups, or some combination of the two.

But loosely coupled does not mean unaligned. A loosely coupled idea can adhere to values, competencies, and even policies of its parent while also morphing to meet the market much faster, more

*Mapping the flow of e-mail provides an immediate and up-to-the-minute view of the many forms the organization has taken.*

adeptly, and at lower cost than it could through a monolithic hierarchy.

The biggest challenge in managing this type of organization is to put in place a method for actually mapping interactions between individuals and workgroups. Since there are always many ad hoc teams being built to address new ideas, the way in which these teams communicate one with another can be critical to creating a culture where ideas are not only generated rapidly but also inventoried, recombined, and repurposed. No organization chart can accomplish this.

What I have seen are various forms of social networking approaches used to help individuals within organizations find like-minded associates with whom to develop ideas. IBM has set up such a system internally as part of its Innovation Zone. Employees can use the social network, which is similar to popular public Internet sites such as MySpace and Facebook, to connect with each other. These networks reflect the communities and competencies of an organization, which fall outside any org chart. For example, imagine mapping the flow of e-mail to and from every individual in your organization. This would provide an immediate and up-to-the-minute view of the many forms the organization has taken, without regard to anyone's position, title, or function, providing a solid foundation for collaborative innovation.

Once you identify ideas, create a platform for sharing and collaboration around them, and ultimately bring them to market or put them into practice, you have still only begun the task of innovation. Remember, innovation is a process, and staying in the zone does not end here.

## Innovation Recap

Leadership plays a crucial role in building an Innovation Zone. The role operates chiefly in four areas:

- Separating core competencies from the core business model
- Building and reinforcing a culture of innovation
- Counterbalancing entrenchment in past success
- Creating an organizational structure that facilitates innovation

Pursuing core competency requires a delicate balance between identifying a core competency and challenging the business models put in place to extract value for it. Leaders need to put in place five elements for a culture of innovation to thrive:

- Visibly committed leadership

- Defined area of responsibility

- Rewards

- Customer involvement

- Mentoring and training

Unfortunately, success creates incumbents, who can easily develop tunnel vision as the result of their success. This momentum can make spotting new markets and opportunities nearly impossible, which is why leadership needs to push an organization to keep looking for trends outside its core business model.

The structure of an organization can hinder or accelerate innovation. While more distributed and less hierarchical structures tend to work best for innovation in smaller organizations, this sort of free-form structure is exceedingly difficult to preserve as an organization grows. To counter this, organizations can adopt loosely coupled structures, such as those found in many large service companies. This model allows an organization to act responsively to local as well as enterprise-wide opportunities. The biggest challenge in managing this type of an organization is developing a method for mapping interactions between individuals and workgroups so as to make it easy to create cross-organizational communities based on competencies and knowledge rather than organizational structure.

CHAPTER 4

# INNOVATION 2.0

*Twentieth-century manufacturing developed a rigid mechanism for ensuring the quality, predictability, and reliability of products and services. In that era of new ideas, from lightbulbs to automobiles, the process of coming up with new ideas belonged to brilliant and creative minds, most of whom inhabited laboratories, research and development centers, and academia. Yet innovation can no longer be relegated to one isolated part of the organization or to any one group of people. And it certainly cannot be sustained in any organization without a well-defined context and process.*

What strikes many as odd is that creativity and innovation can coexist with the rigor needed for high quality and can be found in every part of an organization. In fact, they must coexist if an organization or an industry is to thrive and grow. This is the intent of creating the systematic and flexible approach I call "Innovation 2.0."

But to understand how to create Innovation 2.0 and balance these seemingly opposite objectives of creativity and quality, and of focused and diffused innovation, it's necessary to understand how we got where we are today.

## The Birth of the Modern Innovation Lab

In the early seventeen hundreds, exploration and trade—based mostly on travel by sea—were stifled by a problem of immense proportions: Sailors could not determine their location on the globe without the aid of clocks more accurate than any yet built. One of the greatest and first examples of modern-day innovation was waiting in the wings to solve this immense problem.

Global positioning, since the time of the earliest navigators, is a matter of plotting location in terms of latitude, the distance north or south of the equator, and longitude, distance eastward and westward from any given point on the circumference of the globe. Latitude was relative child's play, determined by the position of constellations in the night sky or of the sun. Longitude, however, required a precise measure of the time at a ship's location compared with the time at its port of departure. Compare the two and you know how far you've traveled east or west across the face of the globe.

In 1714 accurate timekeeping was a daunting challenge. Sea merchants had been urging the English Parliament to do something that would spur a solution to the problem of determining longitude. In response Parliament put in place the Board of Longitude, which over the next hundred years disbursed upward of £100,000 for research on the topic.

Ultimately, the problem was solved by an enterprising and astoundingly persistent clockmaker, John Harrison, whose journey of frustration is a parable for anyone whose bright ideas are having difficulty taking root in the structure of a large organization.[1]

*The real innovation was not the product that solved the problem; it was the process put in place to develop it.*

So here's a question for you. What was the innovation? If you're thinking it was Harrison's clock, that's only partially right. Harrison's clock was no doubt a scientific and engineering marvel. But the real innovation was the process Parliament put in place.

In many ways Parliament's approach to innovation ushered in an age of amazing discovery by acknowledging that innovation involves much more than simply applying smart people to a problem. While the Board of Longitude's approach was crude and politically motivated, it did establish a template for fostering new ideas and creating a community of knowledge around a problem that had far greater reach than the conventional scientific process of the time. The board spurred the generation of ideas, fostered collaboration (albeit of the most cutthroat kind), evaluation, risk, experimentation, refinement, and speed of practical application. The effect was not unlike the role that open innovation communities play today.

The centuries since this early precedent for R&D have seen the growth of a deep discipline around science, engineering, research, and development. This evolution of the discipline of R&D has probably been the defining trend of the era from the early 1700s to the present day. And all of that discipline has led to the belief that innovation is what happens when we apply ourselves to the task of focusing on a singular market challenge to deliver a new product or service. That is far from the truth.

Most often innovation ends up involving high measures of serendipity. It's humbling to think of how many modern-day discoveries have involved stumbling over a catalyst. But as Richard Carlton (one of 3M's original directors) once quipped, "We've made a lot of mistakes. And we've been very lucky at times. Some of our products are things you might say we've just stumbled on. But you can't stumble if you're not in motion."

## Where Does Innovation Reside?

Staying in motion is the hardest thing for many companies to do when something is working. Success stalls innovation, leading people to believe that the company can be put at risk by sudden movement. When fear of stumbling sets in, innovation becomes the province of a small group who see their job as protecting the past rather than creating the future. They shelter ideas that have already succeeded, and make little room for new ones.

Which is why when you talk about innovation with most people you will eventually get to the question of where innovation resides in a company. "Innovation has to happen somewhere, right?" people say. "That way we can make sure it's done right and we can protect the best interests of the company. After all, we have places where our accounting, contracts, sales, marketing, technology are all managed; why not innovation?" The simple answer most people come to is that innovation belongs in the research and development, or R&D, function of an organization.

That makes perfect sense in the traditional notion of how an organization runs and how innovation should be done. After all, R&D is where we keep all those very smart, socially challenged, welldegreed individuals who think up bright ideas. So we build labs and research facilities where we can safely house all our smart people and where they can work happily together, periodically spitting out an idea or two that the rest of us can take to market or put in practice.

*Staying in motion is the hardest thing for many companies to do when something is working.*

This is precisely the challenge alluded to in the introduction about the importance of re-innovation, a term used specifically to point out that innovation itself needs to be re-created. Today innovation is often cast in a form that limits its ability to grow an organization by making it the job of just a few. Re-innovation is about taking what used to be confined to the laboratory and making it a competency of the entire organization, from the scientist to the salesperson. Re-innovation is nothing less than the re-creation of innovation as a fundamental discipline that crosses all the boundaries made sacrosanct over the past three hundred years of industry.

If we have anyone in recent history to blame for this notion of innovation as having a home, it is the person who popularized the notion of an innovation laboratory, Thomas Edison. Many feel that Edison's greatest contribution to the twentieth century was not in any of his thousand-plus individual inventions but rather in his creation of the product development laboratory.

The Menlo Park lab that Edison built was the first research lab in the United States. It lasted for only four years, from 1876 to 1880, yet it was the prototype for virtually every other research lab over the next century.

Edison's lightbulb eventually led to the formation of General Electric in 1892. In 1900 GE put in place its first R&D center, in Schenectady, New York, spearheaded by another great inventor, Charles P. Steinmetz. Over the next two decades GE built its research lab into a powerhouse of talented scientists and engineers. It was a centralized and highly coordinated function within GE, and it was also the role model for virtually every other major organization of the day. Companies from around the globe sent their brightest talent to GE to find out how a lab should be set up and run.

The result was a century of nearly identical research labs fashioned after the classic Edison model. The model worked well. It still does. But it also pigeonholed the idea of innovation as something that resided within the R&D function of an organization.

"What's wrong with that?" you might ask. Well, think about the simple example of innovation on the Internet. How many of the Web sites you use today came out of a large R&D lab? If high-powered R&D is the source of new ideas, then Google, YouTube, Facebook, Amazon.com, and eBay all should have been invented by major players. None was!

Has something changed fundamentally in how we innovate? Why aren't the major players the ones who are changing the world today? Well, as Drucker used to say to me, "perhaps it's the wrong question." It's not that R&D is dead. Far from it. We still need smart people in medicine, engineering, and science to help solve many of the complex problems facing the world. But we also find ourselves being able to tap into a new and much more expansive group of ideas that can come at any time from virtually any corner of the globe. The challenge is not to move away from R&D but rather to expand the notion of what R&D is and what it applies to. As with the idea markets discussed in chapter 5, this also creates a new economic formula for research that allows us to pursue outlier ideas by shifting the economic burden to the market rather than leaving it entirely on the shoulders of the organizations seeking solutions.

But now back to the original question: Where does the innovative capacity and capability of your organization reside?

## Innovation 2.0

In the appendix you will find a scaled-down version of the assessment I've used with more than three hundred organizations to help them determine how well equipped they are for innovation and where their innovation comes from. Compressed as it is, it can give you a sense of where your organization stands. But it is possible to scale down the assessment still further; you can take a quick litmus test of the ability to foster innovation across an organization with one simple question. Consider the following situation:

> An accountant in the finance department stumbles across an unaddressed market demand that the company is well suited to support. The company loves the idea, and the accountant excitedly sets to work to try it out.

*How realistic is this scenario of innovation in your organization?* Amazingly, your answer to this simple question is one of the most telling indicators of innovative capability. In hundreds of surveys that I've conducted over more than a decade's time now, the answer to this question is the most closely related to an organization's ability to rank well on most other aspects of innovation!

The accountant scenario seems to cut to the core of why many company cultures dismiss ideas not generated by designated thought leaders. Ideas are suppressed rather than encouraged and nurtured. Innovation is not a matter of encouraging ideas among those already expected and paid to come up with new ideas—it is a matter of encouraging and accepting these ideas wherever they may appear.

*Just as central R&D had to be developed and institutionalized over the past two hundred years, we now need a new function to cultivate ideas from throughout the organization.*

But here lies one of the most basic challenges for companies trying to encourage innovation. Just how do you handle this sort of volume of new ideas? It's especially hard when many of them are indeed off the wall and have little relevance to an existing way of doing business.

Shutting these ideas off too early and too often will just discourage people, resulting in the effective suppression of new ideas. Allowing all of them to make their way into the business will quickly overwhelm any organization.

This points to the flaw in the innovation model used today in most organizations, which is built to generate ideas from one place, R&D. An idea that starts there will be taken seriously, evaluated through some methodical processes, and then tested and, if it makes it through the right gates, ultimately commercialized. But ideas that start elsewhere have no path to follow. In fact, they typically have nothing but obstacles to contend with. In this respect we are stuck in a 1920s-style division of labor that is woefully outdated for today's demands.

Just as central R&D had to be developed and institutionalized over the past two hundred years, we now need a new function to cultivate ideas from throughout the organization.

## CENTERS OF GRAVITY FOR INNOVATION

This is precisely what many leading-edge organizations are doing by putting in place a center of gravity for innovation. These innovation teams are sometimes on call to seek out new ideas and help their owners to identify ways to evaluate and test them. Alternatively, the innovation team may operate as an independent internal investment group, watching for new ideas and helping shape them early in their life cycle. This model was popularized by Xerox's PARC lab, which in the 1990s established a ventures group, Xerox New Enterprises (XNE), to develop a series of new technologies for the Web. While PARC had always been a powerhouse of innovative ideas, it had also been widely criticized for not being able to commercialize ideas—notably the graphical user interface popularized as Microsoft Windows. The intent of XNE was to capitalize on these ideas by separating them from Xerox and allowing them to flourish as independent companies.

Another model that is increasingly being adopted by large organizations is that of having an internal group whose exclusive focus is the development of new ideas. These groups are typically unaligned with any other function in the organization, such as R&D, engineering, marketing, or sales. Instead, as in the Partners HealthCare example, they are self-contained units that have all the resources needed to evaluate and fund a new idea and bring it to market. Unlike the XNE model at Xerox, these are internal business units who work intimately with other internal groups and actively promote an outreach program for new ideas. These teams go to great lengths to avoid any perception of ownership over new ideas; instead, they act as facilitators and advocates of the ideas. This is an especially interesting model for one overwhelming reason: It divorces the idea from the budgeting constraints and limitations that would otherwise force the idea's creator to abandon it for lack of resources.

## BUDGETING AS AN INNOVATION KILLER

Again it is the organizational model, in this case the processes of budgeting for the known rather than the unknown, that inhibits innovation. Budgets are put in place to accommodate anticipated needs. But budgets can't accommodate unknown opportunities. This fundamental flaw in the finances of large organizations largely explains the way start-ups overtake incumbents, and the way incumbents respond by attempting to acquire start-ups rather than build competing operations for themselves. It is easier for the vast majority of organizations to justify acquiring new ideas that have already been built

*If the market rewards an acquisition of a successful player more than it does experimentation in new markets, what self-respecting, stockholder-accountable CEO wouldn't take that path?*

into successful businesses than to build new products or services for themselves, even though the price is many times higher.

It seems perverse that this would be the case, but in an odd way it is this phenomenon that has so dramatically spurred the vast majority of new companies in every industry. Incumbents lack neither the brainpower nor the inherent intellectual capability to come up with new ideas, but they typically have no mechanism in place, other than R&D, by which to fund these ideas once they emerge.

Keep in mind that an economy where buy-rather-than-build organizational behavior is common offers little incentive to change the behavior. I recall a conversation I once had with Larry Ellison, CEO of software giant Oracle, where we were talking about the merits of trying to educate a market on a major new software technology trend. I suggested to him that Oracle had a significant opportunity to step into a new market by creating a campaign to raise the visibility of a new genre of software. His response was that he'd rather not take that step if another company, in this case a smaller start-up, could do it. Then, when the market was sufficiently educated and had bought into the new start-up's business and validated its worth, Oracle could always acquire the company. The comment took me by surprise at first, but as I thought about it I had to admit, why not? If the market rewards an acquisition of a successful player more than it does experimentation in new markets, what self-respecting, stockholder-accountable CEO wouldn't take that path?

Which is why it's critical that larger organizations have a high level of competency around mergers and acquisitions in order to purchase innovation by buying companies that have already built innovative processes, services, and products. This is simply the reality of the market.

## Creating an Innovation 2.0 Portfolio

In the end companies need to optimize behavior to satisfy both the short and long view of the marketplace. It's just not enough to cater to the whim of analysts who look at quarterly performance as the sole indicator of well-being. A balance has to be created that acknowledges both the short and long view. One approach to help strike this sort of balance between short- and long-term innovation objectives is to use a framework for establishing an innovation portfolio, which will help in creating both an understanding of where and how an organization makes innovation investments. The portfolio also provides an ongoing road map for leaders, associates, and outside stakeholders to appreciate an organization's approach to innovation.

## TYPES OF INNOVATION

A frequent point of debate on the topic of innovation is the difference between breakthrough and continuous innovation. For many, innovation only counts when it falls into the breakthrough category. Others believe that breakthrough innovations are nothing more than a series of incremental innovations connected over long periods of time. So fervent is the debate around these two apparent extremes that a religion seems to have formed around each point of view.

The reality is that innovation need not be polarized at either extreme. It is instead a portfolio of investments across this spectrum.

In its purest form innovation is the creation of value through some change in a product, service, or process. The change may be significant and unexpected or it may be slight and predictable. As long as measurable value has been added, both cases are innovative.

*The synthesis of component innovations into radical innovation is one of the most interesting aspects of human progress.*

But it doesn't stop there. Innovation can also be either component based or systemic. Component-based innovation refers to value that is added to one part or aspect of a larger product or process. One of Apple's Distinguished Scientists once talked with me about the iPhone and the tremendous innovation required in algorithms and mathematics to drive the iPhone's ergonomics. These were innovations no one would ever see, yet they were essential components of its appeal. On the other hand, when Motorola introduced the cell phone in 1983 it ushered in a systemic innovation, a fundamental change in how people behave and experience the world through mobile telecommunications.

So which is more important? It's tempting to vote for radical innovation, but don't be too quick to jump to conclusions. Virtually any radical innovation you might look at required dozens if not hundreds of invisible but essential component-based innovations before it could take off. The synthesis of component innovations into radical innovation is one of the most interesting aspects of human progress. Components are typically not invented with a particularly broad purpose, if any, in mind. Most of what passes for innovation is in fact random invention. These are ideas that turn into a tangible item, be it a patent, drawing, or physical object, but have little discernible impact until they find their way into a new product, service, or process. Some of what we today consider to be the most important innovations of the twentieth century started as curiosities with no home.

Gene Meieran, one of Intel's handful of Senior Fellows, told me that the invention of the transistor and the subsequent move toward integrated circuitry was viewed by its creators as interesting but not necessarily world changing.

> At Fairchild we used to have these Wednesday technical reviews and you'd have Andy Grove, Bob Noyce, Gordon Moore, and Herb Kroemer and a whole bunch of people that were talking about this new technology and you'd bring in the faculty from Berkeley and Stanford—Jim Gibbons, Dave Hodges, and all those people—and it was tremendously exciting. But you never really felt that "Goodness, this is going to change the world in a few years" in the way that it has obviously changed the world.

It's easy to confuse this sort of invention with the very intentionally driven radical innovations that components ultimately become part of. One of the classic examples is the mandate given by JFK in 1963 to put a man on the moon before the end of the decade. There is probably no better example of how a single accomplishment embodied countless component-based innovations. As Meieran says,

> There's a big difference between Kennedy's challenge and Moore's challenge. Kennedy made his challenge, this dream of a big vision, a doable but a stretchable vision that is possible to execute but will take a lot of effort, a lot of discovery, and a lot of innovation and invention. Kennedy did that as a reaction to the "missile gap" and the "space gap" that the Russians had posed. In other words, there was a distinct threat and we needed to figure out how we were going to meet that threat. That was the same thing that happened with the Manhattan Project in the development of the A-bomb and the development and manufacturing of the B-29 Superfortress. It's the same thing that happened when the Germans created V1 and V2 rockets. There is a known

threat and you try to meet it. Moore's Law is more of an opportunity. Moore said, "Gee, this is an interesting thing, this periodic doubling of the number of components we can put on a single chip of silicon. I don't know what we're going to do with all these transistors, but we certainly can make them, and inventive people will figure out what to do with them." And so it's been more of a challenge for an opportunity than was the case with Kennedy, where the challenge was to respond to a known threat, to close the space gap.

Meieran's observations really cut to the chase, explaining why so much of innovation passes under the radar. What we most often see and interpret as innovation is only the spectacular result of innovation (an airplane, a man walking on the moon, and so on), not the guts and gore, the many pieces that must be developed to support it. The problem, of course, is how to foster the creation of components when we don't necessarily understand what payoff they will have. The answer is to accelerate the rate at which we can both discover component innovations and reconstitute them into new products, services, and processes, which ultimately reflect and publicize the big innovation everyone sees and admires.

To do that we need to first rethink the way in which we talk about innovation.

## Moving to Innovation 2.0

The idea behind the Innovation 2.0 framework took shape as I was talking to the organizations I worked with in the Center for Business Innovation at Babson College. In our discussions, people would inevitably express concern over the fact that innovation was often considered an undifferentiated task.

In other words, there was no distinction between tactical and radical, or component and systemic innovations. They were all just thrown into a big bucket of new ideas competing against each other for the same resources. The other theme that came up repeatedly was that some companies were simply better equipped to deal with one type of innovation than the other. However, they all compared themselves to the benchmark of radical innovation as the measure of successful innovation. That might work for an Apple Computer, but it

FIGURE 4. **INNOVATION 2.0: AN OVERVIEW**

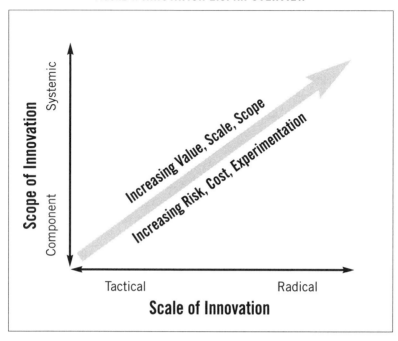

The Innovation 2.0 framework provides a way to categorize different types of innovation across a scale spectrum from tactical to radical and a scope spectrum from component to systemic. The framework represents a continuum of innovations ranked against both dimensions, rather than a clear demarcation differentiating one type of innovation from another.

does not work for a Bank of America, which encounters and depends on many more incremental innovations to improve its services.

One way to characterize the types of innovations that span this spectrum of an innovation life cycle is to use the matrix in Figure 4. This illustrates the way in which innovation can occur along both dimensions, that is, from tactical to radical and from component to systemic. An innovation such as the radio may well be in the upper right extreme of this framework. However, the portable radio could be a radical/component innovation and the transistor on which it is based a tactical/component innovation.

On the other hand, companies that can influence significant shifts in market behavior should consider putting resources into acquiring component innovators rather than trying to build component innovations themselves.

FIGURE 5. **INNOVATION 2.0: FORMS OF INNOVATION**

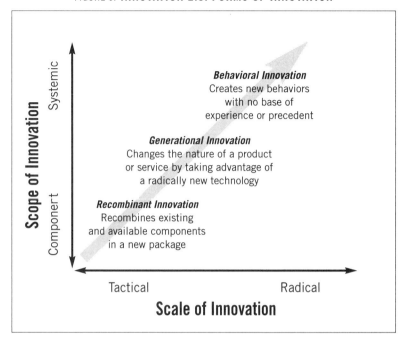

*Innovation can take many forms, reflecting a portfolio of investments in innovation.*

As shown in Figure 5, each of the various stages of an innovation life cycle has a different objective. These objectives fall into three distinct categories:

- Recombinant innovation

- Generational innovation

- Behavioral innovation

Figure 6 shows how the complete portfolio creates a virtuous cycle where innovations feed off one another. What is especially interesting about this is that not only do tactical/component innovations feed upstream innovations but systemic/radical innovations also provide downstream fuel for lesser innovations. But it gets even more interesting. We can easily imagine successful systemic/radical innovations resulting in many new derivative innovations at the component/tactical level.

FIGURE 6. **INNOVATION 2.0: A VIRTUOUS CYCLE**

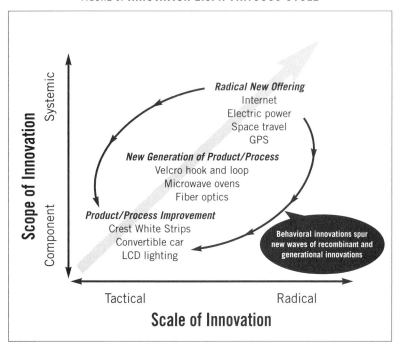

*The complete portfolio creates a virtuous cycle where innovations feed off one another.*

But what if the systemic/radical innovation flops? Do derivative innovations still follow? Absolutely, but only if the flop is quickly dissected and used as a learning experience.

## Quick Case: The Edsel

Perhaps the most famous example of productive failure is the Ford Edsel, which—although a flop of epic proportions—was loaded with component innovations that found their way into future Ford automobiles and manufacturing processes. The Edsel's fate also taught Ford that manufacturing needed to be a separate, cross-divisional activity rather than the division-specific system that led to Mercury employees' grudgingly building the Edsel, resulting in inferior quality. Ford also learned to be more outward facing in understanding market trends, as the Edsel's size and cost both worked against it with the U.S. economy in a downturn. All these were lessons that Ford used well in the launch of the Mustang just a few years later. In this respect the failures of the Edsel were as valuable to the process of innovation as any success. In fact, decades later Saturn's first CEO, Skip LeFauve, is said to have started the launch of what became one of the most successful new car brands by handing out copies of books on the Edsel failure to each of his executives as required reading on what *not* to do!

## Using the Innovation 2.0 Portfolio

Once you have a sense of what your organization's innovation portfolio looks like, the next step is to start asking certain questions about how best to build on your ability to innovate.

First, start with a blank portfolio model and think about the various innovations that your organization is involved with. Where does each one fit? For example, are you creating innovative value through tactical or component efforts? What about ways you are recombining existing inventions to create new innovation? Are there catalysts on the horizon that may offer opportunity for radical and systemic innovation? This exercise is one you should revisit constantly to create a dynamic inventory of all the inventions, combinations, behaviors, market dynamics, and competitive factors that impact your organization's innovation portfolio. In fact, try to create an innovation portfolio for your competitors from your customers' point of view. In some cases I've even gone so far as to have customers fill out the portfolio based on how they perceive an organization. The insights can be remarkable and surprising.

To help you through this exercise, Table 1 provides a grid to fill in your innovation portfolio.

Once you've filled out your portfolio, start to think about how each level of innovation from the lower left to the upper right quadrant feeds off the others. Are there areas where your innovation portfolio is especially strong? Can you use these somehow to build new value and to move toward opportunities that might have greater payback? Are there areas where you are particularly weak, such as combinations of existing components and tactics? This effort creates a rich discussion you can use to establish a common understanding of your organization's innovation capability and focus. In many organizations this portfolio is as essential in navigating how, where, and why

## TABLE 1. **THE INNOVATION PORTFOLIO**

| | Tactical | Strategic | Radical |
|---|---|---|---|
| Systemic | | | |
| Modular | | | |
| Component | | | |

innovation occurs as an organization chart is in identifying responsibilities and capabilities.

Keep in mind that over time radical and systemic innovations can fade into components of next-generation innovations. Take Google's search engine business, which was clearly positioned in the upper right quadrant just a few years ago. Today search is a strategic building block for a new generation of business models that extract value from the combination of search with other things such as radio, calendaring, desktop applications, and GPS. At some point—soon—search will be a small tactical component in Google's innovation portfolio, requiring the identification of new catalysts and market trends that can spur the next generation of radical systemic innovations.

*True innovation runs in both directions, ultimately shaping the market as much as the market shapes innovation.*

This sort of portfolio approach to discussing, evaluating, and prioritizing innovation is far broader than the traditional notion of R&D. It focuses on a wide set of issues that include the nature of every aspect of the business, from the smallest pieces of the technology to the largest trends in an industry and the marketplace.

But why stop here? If you are building a truly open portfolio that reaches out to every part of your organization, shouldn't it also stretch beyond the organization and into the marketplace? Absolutely! And that's the topic of the next chapter. As I've already said, innovation is collaboration between the market and the provider. True innovation runs in both directions, ultimately shaping the market as much as the market shapes innovation.

## Innovation Recap

Chapter 4 focuses on how the modern notion of an R&D lab evolved from its very early beginnings in the 1700s to Thomas Edison's nineteenth-century Menlo Park lab and its growth into the GE model replicated across the world in the twentieth century. This model of innovation as a separate and often isolated function has resulted in the notion that all innovation must come from R&D, a belief that stifles innovation in other parts of the organization.

The Innovation 2.0 framework is a core model that explains the various forms of innovation, from incremental and component to radical and systemic. Every change that adds value across this spectrum qualifies as innovation, not just the sort of radical change commonly regarded as innovative. The Innovation 2.0 framework also illustrates how the spectrum of innovations from an ecosystem of ideas can be captured and mined continuously. Sometimes even failed radical innovations, such as the infamous Ford Edsel, can be decomposed into numerous incremental and component innovations as well as lessons that become the cornerstones of future generations of successful innovation.

CHAPTER | 5

# OPEN-MINDED INNOVATION

*The innovative organizations are the ones that can quickly depart from their planned trajectory and jump onto a new opportunity. It is ultimately the speed with which they do this and their willingness to experiment in new and unanticipated areas that determine the extent to which their innovation is open, that is, subject to influence by factors that are both unknown and unknowable. No amount of time or information will increase the certainty or orderliness of innovation. Instead, innovation must involve openness to disruption, risk, and uncertainty, and must both allow for these factors and employ them rather than shy away from them.*

One of the topics most often discussed in the field of innovation is the shift from an inside function to one that involves customers, partners, and suppliers. Often called "open innovation," this concept is not necessarily radical in itself.[1] After all, markets have always been the drivers of innovation in most industries. It is also not a new phenomenon. Although the term did not appear until 2003, many companies were moving full steam ahead with open innovation well before that. For example, consider NordicTrack, which pioneered its idea in the early 1990s. Although 1993 was well before the Internet,

NordicTrack had no problem getting new ideas. It solicited inventors through classified ads in the back of magazines such as *Popular Science* and *Design News*. As a result, NordicTrack was getting about a hundred invention submissions a week, ranging from sketches on cocktail napkins to complete CAD files and multimedia presentations.

## Letting the Outside In

Genuine open innovation is less about drawing hard lines around internal versus external and more about creating processes that have inherent permeability. If Sony's Akio Morita had asked customers to design the first Walkman, it never would have come into existence. *Open* also implies an element of uncertainty, randomness, and risk designed into the innovation process. For example, when pilots hone their skills by training in flight simulators, they don't just fly in predictable situations—they face randomized weather problems and mechanical malfunctions. They won't necessarily encounter the same conditions in the air, but their ability to deal with and improvise in the face of the unknown improves when they are exposed to higher degrees of uncertainty. The same applies to innovation. If we stick to a single stream of ideas and never create churn to disrupt that flow, we will not be adept at spotting and taking advantage of new trends, opportunities, and options when they make themselves available.

*It's as though we develop such conviction in our ability to predict what's to come that we refuse to take a detour into reality when we run directly into it.*

A lot of people have difficulty with this aspect of open innovation. From having seen organizations consistently struggle with this, I can't help concluding that we want to take far too much credit for being able to see into the future rather than marshal our resources as needed when we actually encounter the future! It's as though we develop such conviction in our ability to predict what's to come that we refuse to take a detour into reality when we run directly into it.

In large part this was the choice for LEGO, the producer of LEGO brand toys, when its users started to hack into its Mindstorms robot kits. After years of struggling to maintain control over the hijacked product, LEGO finally realized that what it had been treating as a disruption was in fact a dedicated and enthusiastic global community of developers that could be tapped to deliver new products. Today LEGO has extended the philosophy to its online LEGO Factory, which allows users to build personalized kits and share them with others. My son Adam is forever creating his own LEGO toys using what looks to me like sophisticated Web-based computer-aided design software. To Adam it's just a cool way to play with LEGOs without having to clean up the mess afterward. LEGO's latest robotic creation, NXT Mindstorms, was in large part developed through this sort of open cooperation with users.

The LEGO phenomenon is hardly an isolated one. Many developers of computer games and game consoles have started to open their environments to users. Sony provides users of its Playstation consoles with a program they can use to customize their Playstation with their own games. Many look to the model of open source, which was popularized as a means to allow vast communities of software developers to create sharable free software, as a template for how communities can establish a network of continuous innovators. Open source has come under severe criticism by many as an unreliable, low-quality alternative to purchased software, but the movement has flourished, in large part because the value proposition for software has itself changed radically. The speed with which new software solutions can be developed in an open source model is without comparison. This is not because any single individual is able to step in and develop a new innovation but because of the organic nature with which hundreds and thousands of individuals can build on one another's efforts using a common and standardized platform.

*The point is not to simply motivate individuals to submit ideas but to motivate them to build on one another's ideas. The two are worlds apart in terms of the difficulty to implement and the value delivered.*

This ability to *crowdsource*, as it was popularly termed by Jeff Howe in a June 2006 *Wired* magazine article,[2] is hardly a new idea. In fact the early 1700s Board of Longitude, described in chapter 4, was one of the earliest examples of crowdsourcing on a significant scale. What clearly makes today's crowdsourcing different is the ability to instantly access and build on the ideas of others. It is this element of open innovation that is too often overlooked by many companies trying to enable it. The point is not to simply motivate individuals to submit ideas but to motivate them to build on one another's ideas. The two are worlds apart in terms of the difficulty to implement and the value delivered. By the way, crowdsourcing is not just about individuals; it is just as important to acknowledge the role of groups and other enterprises in a crowdsourcing model.

## Not Everything Is Open

At the same time, not all systems should be open. Security, regulatory issues, and risk can simply make openness impossible. JetBlue may be able to innovate in the experience of air travel through its leather seats, a bit more legroom, edgy culture, and seatback DirectTV, but it won't soon change the way planes get you from point A to point B. That doesn't mean you can't innovate in air travel or that someone else, perhaps Virgin Galactic, might not actually change the way we are transported about the globe, but you had better understand which aspect of innovation you have the latitude to change within your business and which will require a radically new model. It's the reason BMW made great strides early in the introduction of the Mini Cooper by separating the BMW core brand from the Mini brand. It's also the reason VW's $80,000 Phaeton luxury brand failed, dragged down by the strong attachment of VW to the notion of an affordable car for the people. Creating distance between a core brand and a new business can significantly help create an Innovation Zone where risk and uncertainty do not threaten the core brand and therefore the company can more readily afford experiments and fast failures. It can also distance the innovation team from any defensive culture in the organization.

*A mountain of ideas can end up being a monumental problem.*

For practical purposes it's important to acknowledge that many systems, such as accounting or legal, are closed and can be adequately dealt with through probability and predictability. Being open about the way you innovate does not mean you need to expose your books and legal standing to excessive risk. At the same time, however, remember that in the future fewer and fewer systems will be closed—and therefore more will be subject to uncertainty. The reason for the increase in open systems stems from what I call *technology entanglement,* which is nothing more than the increasing capacity of networking technologies to integrate otherwise disparate and separate systems and also increase their transparency. No matter how hard anyone may try to stem the tide, transparency in nearly every aspect of modern organizations and personal life is increasingly putting us all under constant scrutiny in areas where we don't necessarily invite or embrace scrutiny.

Accepting this fact of life and identifying ways to benefit from the transparency is one way to offset the near-term discomfort of working under glass.

## Playing the Numbers

As noted earlier, open innovation is not just a numbers game. Many people believe that innovation is simply a matter of creating more ideas. If one good idea comes out of a hundred, they think, then ten good ideas will come out of a thousand. That math is one-sided. It reminds me of my nine-year-old saying that if he makes one dollar selling ten glasses of lemonade on the street corner then he'll sell ten million glasses and make a million dollars. It doesn't take long to see the problem here! There's a lot of infrastructure that goes into selling that much lemonade, which quickly erodes your profit margin, not to mention the traffic backup at the lemonade stand! The same is true for filtering new ideas. A mountain of ideas can end up being a monumental problem. You'll upset those who submit the ideas when you can't get back to them, you'll drown in the processes of evaluating each new idea, and you'll end up with a stockpile of ideas that just can't be applied to any particular problem at hand.

Open innovation needs to be taken as seriously as any other investment in the creation of new ideas, and perhaps even more seriously. It involves creating linkages with customers and partners that cross the line from external to internal, opening windows into your own processes of innovation.

## Working the Problem

Open innovation works best when you have a problem on hand that you can articulate and that requires some reasonable degree of understanding of the field. That may seem counterintuitive. After all, isn't the reason for opening the innovation process to get an outside point of view that isn't stuck in the same old way of looking at the problem?

It's tempting to romanticize innovation by expecting it to be a completely democratic process. That's the view embodied in the classic urban myth of the truck wedged under a low overpass in heavy traffic. While firefighters, police, and sundry other experts try to dislodge the truck with heavy equipment, a small child comes upon the scene and suggests someone let the air out of the tires. Everyone is dumbfounded by the suggestion, which of course works, making the child a hero—the apparent moral being that we get dumber in our need to overcomplicate solutions as we get older. That moral certainly contains more than a grain of truth, but a dose of common sense is also in order.

*One of the biggest challenges of open innovation is in somehow capturing accidental knowledge and connecting it to intentional efforts.*

The challenge with many innovations is not so much in finding the idea for an innovation but actually putting it into practice. This inevitably means getting people to accept the idea, experiment with it, and take the risk of adopting it. Those three simple steps often require overcoming a fortress of defenses from incumbents who have far more to lose by admitting personal defeat than they have to gain by accepting organizational success. Think about that the next time you see a good idea and wonder why no one has accepted it, or at least tried it.

## Unintentional Innovation

In many cases innovation happens when we stumble upon something that is completely ancillary to our original mission; it's not necessarily a matter of intent at all. In an open innovation model you need to provide incentives. But how do you then foster the discovery of accidental knowledge that may not have been part of the problem you were trying to innovate a solution to? You can't. One of the biggest challenges of open innovation is in somehow capturing this accidental knowledge and connecting it to intentional efforts. If a pharmaceutical scientist researching hypertension control discovers a compound that grows an extra tail on mice while trying to cure their hypertension, will it be seen as an annoying side effect or a new opportunity? Well, it probably depends on the researcher's employer's reward system. If it's based on the number of compounds discovered to reduce hypertension, you can rest assured that the side effect will be no more than a speed bump on the road to success—not a hot prospect for the traumatic injury team.

These sorts of accidental discoveries will only increase over time as the store of accumulated knowledge also increases. And, in the spirit of open systems, this is knowledge available to an ever-increasing number of individuals and with a shorter and shorter shelf life. Another way to look at this is that what we know is increasing rapidly as measured in terms of volume (number of books, pages of research, Web sites, and so on), but it is increasingly a smaller percentage of what we need to know to deal with the ultimate open system of the marketplace.

Some companies are starting to make headway in how they balance the many elements of open innovation. In each case the common thread is the dramatic way in which open innovation changes the fundamental economic tenets of traditional models of R&D.

## Case Study: Precor's High-Impact Innovation

Walk into any health club and you are greeted by a whirling maze of high-tech equipment designed not only to keep you fit but also to keep you comfortable and entertained. However, it wasn't always that way. Throughout the twentieth century most of the equipment used in gyms and health clubs was unwieldy, bulky, and downright uncomfortable. After all, a workout was supposed to be painful, so what was a little discomfort to boot? That image of fitness began to change at many points as the industry and health consciousness matured, but one of the most significant developments began with a chance encounter at a cocktail party in 1980.

David Smith, an enterprising young engineer and industrial designer, was mingling at a party when he was approached by a U.S. distributor of a European supplier to the fitness industry. The man asked him if he could help fix a popular European rowing machine and repurpose it for the home exercise market. At the time rowers were becoming a workout staple at most health clubs but notorious for their lack of a "user-friendly" interface and subject to constant breakdowns. Besides, many of them looked as though they would be more at home in a medieval dungeon than a health club. This particular machine's manufacturer was just looking for a few quick fixes that would tweak the design, hardly the stuff of innovation. David wasn't inspired by the proposition but did offer an alternative: "Let me start from scratch and I'll design an entirely new rower!"

*"Let me start from scratch and I'll design an entirely new rower!"*

David got the job and proceeded to create a rower that defied all conventional wisdom. His machine was a world removed from its predecessors. It included radical new equipment, new welding techniques, a lightweight aircraft-grade anodized aluminum frame, a comfortable seat, and user-designed ergonomics, and it promised to hold up to the most severe use and abuse.

The design was a hit, and David soon found himself responsible for the Amerec 610, a rowing machine that reshaped the fitness industry and brought rowing to the forefront of fitness. By 1984 the Precor brand had been formed and the company introduced additional rowers, a couple of stationary bikes, and a treadmill, all sporting new microprocessor-based electronics that provided continuous feedback to users.

During the next ten years, the Precor brand spread through sales to individuals, setting a new standard for novelty, quality, and durability. Yet the real prize was to break into the commercial fitness center market, a much more demanding playing field but also a much more lucrative one. The problem was that Precor simply didn't have a unique offering. In a market that many considered mature and stable, the incumbents had the edge with their relationships, branding, and supply chains.

But Precor had a benefit. It was open to ideas from the outside. After all, it was in its DNA from the outset, when it was the outsider. It had already proven the market wrong with David's rower and it was wired to recognize opportunity. Which is exactly what it did in 1987.

At an industry trade show three Precor executives, Jim Birrell, Bill Pots, and Paul Byrne, decided to use their lunch hour to visit an aspiring inventor who had set up a demo of a new idea in a hotel room on the outskirts of Chicago—in the hopes that someone might take an interest. Jim and his team arrived to see an odd contraption cobbled together from a four-by-four wood post, old exercise bike parts, rubber plumbing and tubing, and other assorted odds and ends. Precor was not the first company to look at the device; but while others had decided that it was hardly the stuff of innovation, the Precor team knew at once that something about the crude prototype showed real potential. Others saw the device as crude and easily dismissed it; the Precor team moved fast. Their DNA for innovation helped them understand the value of a good idea, even if it didn't fit the prescribed pattern for what already existed at the time.

*Inventors are driven by a different set of desires and ambitions from the ones that drive innovators. Both may seek fortune, but what drives them and what allows them to sustain invention and innovation are not the same.*

The inventor, Larry Miller, had built the device for his daughter, a fanatical exerciser. She loved the fitness benefits of running but really suffered from the negative impact on her joints. After hearing her complain a few times, Larry set out to see what he could come up with. He went so far as to have his wife drive him around behind her as she ran through the neighborhood, and with a camcorder he taped his daughter's running. (You have to wonder what the neighbors were thinking.) Later Larry would play the tape back in slow motion on the family TV and recorded his daughter's foot movements on the screen with a magic marker!

Of course, she had other options for staying fit, but none simulated the motion of running without the impact. Treadmills cushioned the shock with softer surfaces, but for joints that were already compromised the pain and damage continued and worsened. Cross-country trainers were better but these also put excessive strain on knees and hips.

Larry spent months studying runners from every angle, paying attention to the finest nuances of how they moved and flexed. Finally he realized that he could simulate running without the impact forces runners had to endure. Larry's solution was elegant, simple, and incredibly effective—so much so that you'd be hard-pressed twenty years later to find a health club without his innovation: the elliptical trainer. The elliptical trainer allows a full range of motion, a full body workout, and all the benefits of running with none of the impact.

*Far too many organizations are simply not open to outside ideas. Due to paranoia, legacy, or just plain arrogance they shut the doors to outside invention.*

When the Precor team saw that first crude elliptical trainer, none of that was lost on them. They signed a letter of intent with Larry on the spot. The cultural DNA involved in that moment of insight, in the transition from invention to innovation, is so subtle as to go unnoticed unless you understand the context and legacy of the story.

Inventors are driven by a different set of desires and ambitions from the ones that drive innovators. Both may seek fortune, but what drives them and what allows them to sustain invention and innovation are not the same. The power of an Innovation Zone, which is exactly what Precor is in the fitness industry, comes from the ability to quickly recognize and monetize ideas. That is a process of operational excellence that defies the psychology of inventors. Inventors on the other hand are driven by a vision of what can be; they see the future in a grain of sand but will rarely if ever ask how to pave the path to get there.

From the outset Precor realized how important this distinction is and how important working with outside inventors can be. Jim Birrell, who was there for the discovery of the elliptical trainer, is now Precor's chief innovation officer. His mission is to help put in place an open innovation model that allows outside parties to submit ideas and collaborate with Precor on new products and services while making the best use of each party's specific skills and competencies.

Birrell looks to create an environment that offers an Innovation Zone for aspiring internal and external inventors with new ideas for products, features, or business processes. The key is to focus on the customer and be open to any innovation that gets you closer to your goal. However, that sounds much simpler in concept than it is in practice. Far too many organizations are simply not open to outside ideas. Due to paranoia, legacy, or just plain arrogance they shut the doors to outside invention. Or worse yet, they work with outside inventors, where the organization holds all the cards and the inventor is lucky even to be invited to sit at the table.

Precor focuses on being a facilitator and a partner in developing the idea rather than being the big brother. For example, if an inventor has to sign a nondisclosure agreement, it will be bilateral, also binding Precor to confidentiality. This is unheard-of in most industries, where a small player or an individual is approaching a much larger organization, hat in hand. This foundation has created a model of continuous innovation that has propelled Precor over the past two decades.

This sort of relationship, and the trust it builds, is the foundation of Precor's open innovation effort. If inventors accept that an innovation partner will act in their best interests, they are much more likely to develop a relationship and share their ideas. There is also an implicit value in the brand that draws an inventor to a relationship. Establishing the brand as one that offers reliability and integrity is key to an inventor, since it provides the best likelihood that a new idea will have a chance for success.

*The one certainty is that the greatest ideas will continue to come from unexpected sources.*

Today, however, Precor faces a whole new set of challenges and competitors. The integration of interactive media into exercise equipment, new devices from Nike and Apple that couple media players with running shoes to deliver customized workouts, and the personalization of fitness through biometrics are setting a new bar for the industry. Fitness is an experience that provides immersion in media, biometric feedback, and personalized training. The experience of working out has migrated to a personalized situation. The latest generation of fitness equipment includes onboard entertainment that's built into the machine so that you can enjoy your favorite episodes of *Oprah* or, as Birrell puts it, "learn while you burn" as you watch the History channel.

Where will this lead? It's still just as difficult to predict as the elliptical trainer was in 1987. Much of the movement forward will be dictated by the changing demographics of more socially networked kids who want gaming and socialization as part of their fitness experience.

The one certainty is that the greatest ideas will continue to come from unexpected sources. Keeping the doors open to these ideas will be essential to innovation. As Birrell says, "Just because it didn't happen between these walls doesn't mean it's not entrepreneurial."

The challenges ahead and the new dimension of experience only increase the need to build even closer bonds with outside innovators by involving them not only in the generation of ideas and their submission but actually integrating them into the processes of innovation. This changes the nature of the relationship and creates new opportunity—not only for Precor but for the outside innovator as well. In this role Precor becomes a conduit and a center of gravity for a vast community of innovators.

## Quick Case: P&G's Innovation Scale

The trend toward open innovation is equally important to companies much larger than Precor. Most notable among these is Procter & Gamble, which has become somewhat of a living example for the open innovation movement.

P&G, however, sees more to open innovation than the conventional notions of market involvement that surround the idea. For P&G, and for organizations of similar scale, open innovation is not just a matter of reaching out to customers; it includes a tightly integrated set of internal functions as well. In the context of openness this may not seem to fit neatly under the rubric of "open." But stop and think about the degree to which large organizations tend to be disjointed and separated by internal bureaucracy. Before integrating customers into a process, most large companies would be well advised to simply reach out to the wealth of knowledge and wisdom locked behind their own thick divisional and functional walls.

*Far too many organizations jump directly into open innovation with customers and partners, when they would be better served by simply getting their arms around their own sources of innovation.*

P&G chalks up the success of many of its products, such as Crest White Strips and Olay Daily Facials, to this sort of internal openness between otherwise disparate groups. Given the manner in which P&G has grown through a long legacy of acquisitions and its diverse portfolio of brands in more than fifty different categories of products, it's easy to imagine how important the process of open innovation can be within P&G.

I bring this up because far too many organizations jump directly into open innovation with customers and partners, when they would be better served by simply getting their arms around their own sources of innovation.

According to P&G's chief tech officer, Gilbert Cloyd,

> We have over 50 people from all our business units whom we call technology entrepreneurs. These people are very facile in searching both for ideas and for solutions. They attend conventions, form supplier-group networks, and use the Internet.
>
> The Internet has been a major advance for us here. If I've got a problem I've got to solve, or if I have an idea in an area, I can be in touch with someone somewhere around the globe within 24 to 48 hours who has the answer or idea that I need. Neither of us knew each other beforehand. It allows you to exploit the entrepreneurial spirit and the tremendous intellectual capability that exists outside the company. We've now got a palette of virtually unlimited colors.[3]

The goal of all this at P&G is to source 50 percent of new products from outside the organization. That is an astounding number for many organizations to consider. While it may be especially important to do this in a consumer-product organization, you have to wonder to what degree this trend will hold true for other industries. For instance, can you imagine any reasonable percentage of new ideas for products in the aerospace industry coming from outside the organization? What about chemicals? Materials sciences? It may seem absurd at first, but don't be too quick to answer.

## Case Study: InnoCentive Changing the Economics of Innovation

When Alph Bingham was going to school at Stanford, he had a chemistry professor who assigned weekly projects. On the due date this professor would begin the class by writing the names of five students on the board. Each student would then need to come up and defend the work done in the prior week.

What stuck with Alph was that students never had the same solution to any given problem. His conclusion was that it doesn't matter how well trained someone is; people all have extraneous experiences that are going to influence how they approach and solve difficult problems.

Years later Alph founded InnoCentive in an effort to tap this enormous diversity. InnoCentive is an idea marketplace where *seekers and solvers,* to use the innovation vernacular, gather to post challenges and provide solutions. It's a marriage of what he calls a "happily prepared mind" and a problem looking for an innovative solution.

The problems posed on the InnoCentive site often seem to require fairly deep domain expertise in chemistry, physics, engineering, or biology, to name just a few. Yet InnoCentive is constantly surprised by ideas that come in from outside the problem's domain.

Bingham recounts one challenge in the field of polymer chemistry. The company seeking the solutions was pleased with the variety of solutions that came in and decided it wanted to pay for five of the solutions. Among the people who received those awards were an industrial chemist (not too surprising), a veterinarian (that's a little off), a small agribusiness owner, a drug delivery systems specialist, and an astrophysicist!

The initial InnoCentive challenges specified the boundaries of a specific solution and its features. However, that restricted the types of problems that could go up to a narrow list. As the service evolved InnoCentive introduced brainstorming challenges in which seekers were simply looking for the best idea.

One of the points that Bingham makes is that an idea marketplace democratizes innovation by allowing nonexperts as well as domain experts to participate in solving questions. While in many cases the domain experts may well be the best ones to solve a problem in which they have had training and experience, that doesn't mean that

*Idea markets like InnoCentive change the economics of innovation.*

periodically an outsider with far less domain-specific experience but a peculiar perspective and unique insight might not see the problem in a novel way. In any traditional R&D function the focus is on hiring the experts in the field of the problems being solved. Bingham quotes Damon Runyon, author of *Guys and Dolls,* who said, "The race is not always to the swift, nor victory to the strong, but that is how you bet."

Bingham's point is an important one. We all have to place our innovation bets rationally and invest in those areas and people that are most likely to have the answers. No one is suggesting that you stop hiring experts in your field, the "swift" or "strong" who understand the history and legacy of a problem. But there is always an opportunity, however slight, to innovate in a way that may completely defy the experts. With access to a global pool of ideas you bet not only on the swift and the strong but on everyone. It's like trying to place a bet on a horse after it has left the gate—that is, based on its actual performance rather than its track record—which, unfortunately, breaks traditional economic rules on how we can innovate.

The reality is that if any of us had to pick one person we thought most likely to solve a problem, and we were going to pay for time and materials whether the problem got solved or not, we'd pick a Nobel laureate in the problem domain. That's how a reasonable person bets. This creates an economic model around innovation that assumes certain probabilities, risks, and return. However, idea markets like InnoCentive change the economics of innovation. The market assumes the risk, and so the question becomes, Is the cumulative likelihood of solving the problem greater when you involve experts and nonexperts or when you focus just on a few experts? That's a question that's never been viable in the past because it was just not possible to justify the cost of experimenting with everyone, expert or not.

*When you change the economics of how you place your innovation bet, you start to reevaluate who you can afford to place your bet on.*

When you change the economics of how you place your innovation bet you start to reevaluate who you can afford to place your bet on. Still, you have many cultural and social issues to contend with. Few of us trained in any discipline want to believe that a pool of nonexperts, however large, can solve the problem better than we can as experts.

Yet getting over these cultural issues is still only a first step toward realizing the potential of idea markets. That's because in today's idea markets, problem solvers don't know anything about other problem solvers. When a seeker posts a problem to solve, it is solved by an individual or an existing team.

However, there may well be ways to combine novel facets of different solutions in a way that creates a far better overall solution. As InnoCentive and other idea markets evolve, combining solvers into collaborative teams will be one of the biggest breakthroughs in open innovation.

While today's problem-solving teams comprise individuals who share similar interests, disciplines, and perspectives working in the industry, tomorrow's problem-solving teams will combine a multitude of backgrounds and cross-industry disciplines. This approach combines individual problem solvers into teams based on their actual ability to address the diversity of the approaches, rather than a presumption of their ability to solve the problem.

What's especially interesting about InnoCentive's model is that it can also be applied within an organization, challenging the notion of what we mean when we say "open." *Open* does not necessarily mean that the idea has to come from outside the organization. It may just as well come from an employee who might be outside the company's traditional innovators. InnoCentive is already seeing a strong demand for this sort of internal application of open innovation. In large companies that's hardly a surprise, given the sort of silos created to separate different functions and departments.

Whatever the case, be it an internal or an external marketplace of ideas, the point of open innovation is to look at innovation in terms of how it can keep your business model and your market open to new opportunities. If either one is closed, then your ability to innovate is immediately handicapped. In contrast, if you keep both open, you have the chemistry for long-term, sustainable innovation.

## The Ultimate Open Innovation

I've illustrated the impact of the intersection between market and business model openness on innovation in Figure 7. A market model is open if a company extends its products, services, or business model beyond its current market. This may mean that the company extends an existing product to a new demographic. Over time all markets have some openness since the turnover of generations requires the introduction of an existing offering to a new generation of buyers, but the type of openness I mean is proactive and driven by the provider of the offering. Business model openness refers to the degree to which a business extends its services, products, or business model within its existing customer base or market.

For example, when Apple stepped into the music market with its iPod, it moved along the market model axis, creating an entirely new

FIGURE 7. **OPEN AND CLOSED MODELS**

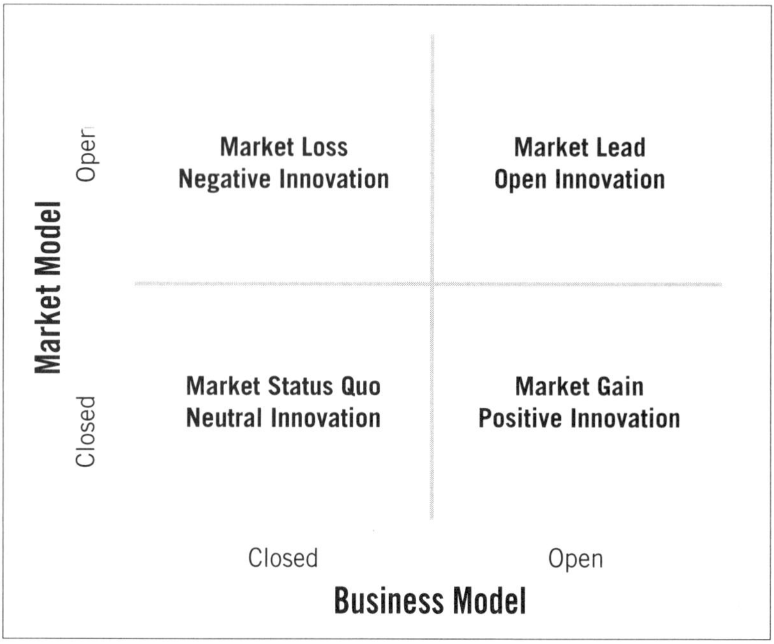

|  | Closed | Open |
|---|---|---|
| **Open** | Market Loss<br>Negative Innovation | Market Lead<br>Open Innovation |
| **Closed** | Market Status Quo<br>Neutral Innovation | Market Gain<br>Positive Innovation |

*Market Model* (vertical axis: Open / Closed)

*Business Model* (horizontal axis: Closed / Open)

*Addressing the opportunities presented by the upper right quadrant, where both the market and business models operate in an open model, can deliver a sustained ability to lead the market.*

marketplace while it also moved along the business model axis through its iTunes music store. This put Apple into the enviable position of the upper right quadrant of the matrix. However, Sony failed to move into a new business model and instead moved vertically into a new market with an existing offering, putting itself into the very risky upper left quadrant. Here's why.

### NEUTRAL INNOVATION

The lower left quadrant of this framework represents the incumbents in any market space. It is where the current business model and market opportunity reside and where the vast majority of near-term opportunity will also appear. There is always room for incremental component-based innovation here. However, an organization that lives solely in this quadrant will slowly slip in its ability to meet the market as the market matures. An incumbent needs to feed on huge volumes of business, which rarely reside outside the lower left quadrant. This means that incumbents will often ignore the merits of other opportunities that lack a near-term payoff. However, these outliers may build significant momentum before an incumbent realizes their value. In some cases, as with Microsoft overtaking IBM in the PC software market and then itself being threatened by Google on the Web, by the time the newcomer is on the radar of the incumbent it's too late to simply acquire the innovation. An open business model can provide warning of such developments well ahead of time. This is exactly what happened to Sony with the iPod. Even though it had the incumbent's advantage in the music business, it was unable to move quickly beyond its existing market and business model, which had been very successful over a long period of time.

## POSITIVE INNOVATION

If a business model is open, then it can occupy the lower right quadrant, positive innovation. Here it is able to retain its market with some minimal innovation and process change directed by its existing customers. These may take the form of a decline in interest for existing products, competitive innovations, or simply new demands from a new set of interests. For example, when Apple introduced its first iPod with five gigabytes of storage for a thousand songs, that was plenty for most users. But as downloading music became easier and the selection of music to download became broader, Apple quickly had to deliver greater storage capacity. The same applies to the introduction of the many generations of iPod, such as the Shuffle and Nano, introduced since the original product. This was hardly a monumental innovation but it did expand Apple's market.

## NEGATIVE INNOVATION

On the other hand, if an organization attempts to address new open market requirements with substantially unchanged products, services, or processes, it has moved into the upper left quadrant of the framework. This quadrant is perhaps the riskiest place to be, so it's the place where you want to spend the least time. When a market does move, your approach will be seen not only as noninnovative but, worse yet, as a failed effort to retain the market

*Think of the open model as a way to help you better understand the dynamics of your capacity to innovate. A high capacity requires both opening the doors to new conversations with the market and expanding the types of markets you are having conversations with.*

with an old business model. This is where Sony ended up in trying to extend its MP3 business to a new market that had already bought into the new business model developed by Apple.

## SUSTAINED INNOVATION

The upper right quadrant reflects the greatest (I would claim the only) avenue for growth and long-term innovation. Here the company and the market both subscribe to an open model of shared insights and collaborative innovation. While some organizations are capable of moving into the upper right quadrant by virtue of their own ability to innovate, as organizations grow this transition becomes harder and harder because of the risk involved. In addition, as an organization grows, the resources it dedicates to the lower left quadrant increase dramatically until they overwhelm its ability to dedicate resources to any other activity. As in the Innovation 2.0 framework, the ideal situation is for an organization to establish a portfolio of processes, products, and services that span the four quadrants.

Think of the open model as a way to help you better understand the dynamics of your capacity to innovate. A high capacity requires both opening the doors to new conversations with the market and expanding the types of markets you are having conversations with. Asking a closed market whether people want something new is likely to yield few new ideas. However, taking the question to a new market could open up opportunities to test ideas with a much more receptive community. Take the case of iRobot, which was quite successful in the space and military marketplace. The idea of a consumer appliance would make little sense to that closed community. You could open up the business model to every single military buyer and still not get a single idea about a consumer product. But open up your market model just slightly and you get a flood of interesting ideas.

Sustained innovation requires this duality of openness on the part of both market and business. Nonetheless, many companies fall short on both counts by trying to hold on too tightly to the products, services, and markets that have served them so well for so long.

## Innovation Recap

Open innovation creates partnerships with outside inventors and makes it possible to use these partnerships to foster innovation.

Despite the benefits of open innovation, however, most large companies would be well advised to tap into the wealth of knowledge and wisdom locked behind their own divisional and functional walls before integrating customers into the process.

Open innovation relies on trustworthiness and partnership to create a new economic model for how to place bets on the sources of innovation. It shifts the burden of invention to a broader community of motivated individuals who have incentives to contribute.

Open innovation can be defined in terms of both the openness of your business model and the openness of your market model. If either is especially reluctant to expand beyond its current way of doing things, then your organization's capacity for innovation is immediately handicapped. If both are open, then you have the chemistry for long-term sustainable innovation.

CHAPTER **6**

# THE SEVEN LESSONS
# OF INNOVATION

*The irony is that innovation is not complex. Organizations that do it well share a common set of behaviors and attitudes. But this is not to say it's easy. Innovation means heavy lifting, but the steps are clear. What I've learned from organizations that have a culture and a track record of successful innovation can be summed up by what I call the seven lessons of innovation. Understanding these and trying to live them on a daily basis is the essential ingredient for staying in an Innovation Zone.*

New ideas need role models. There's no way around the fact that most of us would rather learn from someone else's mistakes and success, even if it means that we will not be able to lead the charge into the future. The risk of paving the way is just too great for the vast majority of rational, levelheaded people to undertake.

Luckily, role models for companies that are building an Innovation Zone do exist.

As I've worked with and studied the companies in this chapter, and many others, it has become clear that the cornerstones of innovation are amazingly similar in each case. Of course, the specific industry, the structure of the organization, its public, private, government, or nonprofit status, and its financial situation do make for differences, but these are slight in comparison to the similarities. I can't give you a formula for innovation that simply allows you to plug in a few numbers and get an answer to how you should innovate—if only it were that easy. But you can apply these seven lessons to the context of your organization as you build an innovative culture.

Keep firmly in mind, as you read through the seven lessons, that each is key to the process of re-innovation. Re-innovation means that

## THE SEVEN LESSONS OF INNOVATION

- Build for the unknown.
- Fail fast.
- Abandon the success of the past.
- Separate the seeds from the weeds.
- Focus on process over product.
- Create an innovation experience.
- Challenge conventional wisdom.

you have created much more than simply a product or service. It means that you have had to re-create and rethink the most basic aspects of how you understood and approached the problem at hand in a way that could never have been anticipated or understood within the limited scope of what had been done up until that point. These seven lessons can help you adopt the kinds of behaviors and culture that will allow you to re-innovate, again and again.

*The seven lessons of innovation are the nuts and bolts of innovation, the elements at the core where the hard work of innovation builds enduring value.*

In this chapter I've synthesized insightful information from what I consider to be some of the best and brightest organizations leading the charge to innovate their businesses and their industries. My samples are by no means an exclusive list; many more organizations are successful innovators. But the ones profiled here cross industries, cultures, and styles of innovation in a way that provides a broad sense of how and why innovation succeeds.

The seven lessons of innovation are meant to be guideposts for any organization considering its own path to an Innovation Zone. They spell out the practical side of innovation, which may not always be glamorous but is always effective. These are the nuts and bolts of innovation, the elements at the core where the hard work of innovation builds enduring value.

Staying in the zone means living by these seven lessons on a daily basis. It sounds easy enough, but each lesson requires committed leadership and an equally committed organization. It is essential to reward and acknowledge individuals and groups for taking the risks involved in maintaining the focus on innovation.

Each of these seven lessons contributes to the ability to innovate in the face of unknown challenges and to quickly reshape an organization to meet fast-approaching obstacles and opportunities. Few areas in the course of human history exemplify that kind of challenge and opportunity as well as the space race of the 1960s.

## Build for the Unknown: NASA and the Space Suit

Like most baby boomers I grew up with the iconic image of space suits. Space suits seemed to be all around us, from the Robinsons' tight-fitting silvery suits in *Lost in Space,* inspired by the original aluminized Mylar-covered Mercury suits, to the gleaming white suits with large gold-tinted bubble helmets worn by the astronauts on the Apollo moon missions.

Today we take for granted the technology of putting humans into space. However, the evolution of the space suit is perhaps one of the most critical innovations that made space flight possible. It's also one of the best examples of innovation in the face of unknowable challenges spanning thousands of individual inventions and six decades of continuous refinement.

With a price tag of $12 million and weighing in at 280 pounds, with its own self-contained propulsion systems, the space suit used today for excursions from the space shuttle is a miniature spacecraft.

When NASA considered putting humans into space, the first space suit developers based the design on the pressurized suits used by military pilots. This worked well enough for early Mercury missions, where the suit was only a backup in the event of a loss of capsule pressure.

*The amazing thing about the space suit is that, like so many great innovations, it was created for circumstances that were mostly unknown.*

However, the obstacles and the stakes mounted quickly during the Gemini program, which set out to conduct the first spacewalk outside a protected and pressurized capsule.

The amazing thing about the space suit is that, like so many great innovations, it was created for circumstances that were mostly unknown. No one could anticipate everything; the suits had to deal with factors the smartest terrestrial scientists could never have known to ask about, but that were immediately obvious once theory met reality.

For example, Ed White, the first person to walk in space, is said to have lost seven pounds in perspiration during that first short spacewalk. Sweat condensation covered the inside of his visor so that he had to feel his way back into the space capsule. To cap it off, his space suit was torn by an external antenna to within one layer, resulting in near catastrophe. It was not something anyone had anticipated. But when his fellow Gemini astronauts had the same issues and nearly passed out from heat and dehydration, it was clear that something was not right. Designers finally figured out the problem. In direct sunlight the temperature of the space suit would spike to 280 degrees Fahrenheit! The air-cooled suits did little to prevent overheating and dehydration. It sounds so simple, but the smartest minds of the day didn't anticipate it. That realization led to the liquid-cooled suits that eventually made landing on the moon possible.

*As what we know about a problem increases, our ability to change decreases.*

This and myriad other challenges, including the fateful tragedy on the Apollo I launch pad (in which Ed White and his fellow astronauts Virgil "Gus" Grissom and Roger Chaffee perished), could only be experienced; they could not be anticipated, no matter how many scenarios and what-ifs were considered.

However, the phenomenon of innovation in the face of such a high degree of uncertainty is not limited to groundbreaking innovation. Any effort to innovate means embarking on a journey of simultaneous learning and change. While we like to believe that both of these will increase, the reality is that—counterintuitive as it may seem—as what we know about a problem increases, our ability to change decreases.

In an enterprise where costs and investments are always measured against some form of benchmark for return or, in the case of a government agency like NASA, the use of allocated funds, learning is not free. Learning requires spending. In the case of air-cooled space suits, tens of millions were spent developing the first-generation suits. Consider that investment the price for a lesson learned—an expensive education, no doubt. The investment also included machines and specialized equipment to build the space suit. You would expect that as the knowledge of how to build a space suit increases you'd be getting closer to your objective. But the investment actually decreases your ability to innovate since each step forward further entrenches you in what may prove to be a failed design.

Every innovation evolves in this manner with less and less leeway to modify its trajectory. It ultimately ends up behaving like a locomotive on railroad tracks.

This attitude of "just do it," despite the cost, may be relatively easy to conceive of in situations where a clear mandate exists to innovate no matter what the risk or odds. But without JFK's oft-quoted mandate to "put a man on the moon before the decade is out," the impediments of the journey to the moon would never have permitted any prudent person to accept the potential downside of such a foolish venture. This is undoubtedly one of the best examples of how leadership alters the perception of risk, allowing an organization to innovate.

This is precisely what innovation, especially radical innovation, needs. Otherwise the risk of uncertainty will always trigger prudence. If it didn't, the vast majority of our minute-to-minute and day-to-day decisions would end up putting us into harm's way—far too much risk for the survival of the species to have ever stood a chance. Periodically, however, prudence and rational argument must give way to intuition, vision, and unfounded conviction. The argument holds true in evolution as well as it does in organizations. The periodic and random mutations that result in the evolution of a species help it to adapt to its environment. These mutations are a necessary part of adapting and surviving. However, not every mutation is a good one. If mutations occur unchecked, you have a cancer. If they are suspended, you have extinction the moment conditions change too much.

The difference between evolution and organizational growth, however, is that evolution has the benefit of immense time frames during which ample latitude is provided for experimentation within a set of known external conditions. Evolution adapts the most fit organisms to the current environment. Organizations, however, must adapt in time frames that require a concerted and conscious effort to change before external conditions are fully present or understood. Without leadership to move things forward despite the unknowable, an organization might stumble into the Innovation Zone, but it will never stay there for long.

As you read through the following cases keep this in mind. Uncertainty dominates the landscape for innovation. Without a concerted effort on your part to inculcate a culture that embraces these seven lessons, you will always be bound by the experiences and success of the past.

## Fail Fast: Sony and the Pocket Radio

I have yet to come across an organization with the ability to sustain innovation that does not also have a deeply rooted culture that encourages experimentation and tolerates failure. This aspect of an innovation culture is immutable; innovation requires tolerance for the right kind of failure. Unfortunately, in many organizations it is just the opposite: All failure is intolerable. To understand this lesson it is necessary to distinguish between acceptable and unacceptable failure—that is, between fast, recoverable failure that is driven by the right motivations and offers an opportunity to learn and failure that is drawn out, creates no residual value for learning, and is motivated by the wrong ambitions.

So, what constitutes an acceptable failure? First, the organization must establish experimentation as a fundamental part of what employees are expected to pursue in their job. At Google, for example, engineers are expected to devote 20 percent of their time on the job to the development of new ideas and products. In an interesting twist on the theme of failure, those engineers who do not find a way to turn that 20 percent into an experiment will receive less favorable ratings than those who do. The expectation is that sustained experimentation will deliver value. Unusual as that approach may be, it's not an innovation; 3M has had a similar program in place for the better part of the company's century-plus existence.

Among the best examples of creating a systemic culture of innovation that relentlessly shunned fear of failure is Sony, one of the great successes of twentieth-century globalization. Its story begins in the ruins of a bombed-out department store in post–World War II Japan.

## A LEAP OF FAITH

As the fourteenth-generation patriarch of his family's sake-brewing business, Kyuzaemon Morita had little doubt as to the fate of his first-born son Akio, who had been groomed to take over the reins. In the aftermath of World War II it is hard to imagine why anyone who had the promise of so much security would choose to do anything else, especially anything that involved high levels of uncertainty and risk. Yet Akio was not as tempted by the trappings of security as he was by the promise of the unknown. He beseeched his father to release him from his obligation so he could start something new, and in an incredible departure from tradition Kyuzaemon not only agreed but invested $25,000 in the new business.

Morita's personal chemistry of defiance and fearlessness in the absence of hard proof, in fact in the face of utter disbelief and ridicule by colleagues and competitors, is the raw material of innovation in its most basic form. Sony's innovations were the foundation of not only an industry but a movement that ultimately led the way to globalization, innovation, and consumerism on a scale more massive than could ever have been conceived of by anyone before World War II.

In 1946, with his father's $25,000 investment and a university colleague named Masaru Ibuka as his partner, Akio formed Tokyo Telecommunications Engineering Corporation (Tokyo Tsushin Kogyo K.K., or TTK).

## TAILOR-MADE INNOVATION

The first big hit for TTK came shortly after Morita licensed the transistor from Western Electric and the patent rights from Bell Labs. He decided to pursue a shirt-pocket-sized radio, which was a huge gamble. Although the transistor had been used with success, and miniaturization was emerging as a trend, no one considered radios personal.

*Morita's first attempt was only a "pocket radio" because he had custom shirts tailored with over-sized pockets for his salespeople!*

However, Morita's first attempt was hardly a pocket radio as we think of it today. In fact, he had custom shirts tailored with oversized pockets for his salespeople so the company could call it a pocket transistor radio! People laughed at him, but he was not dissuaded. He realized that this was something the market had no model for. He understood that there was no way to create a market for the pocket radio without pursuing a series of failed attempts to understand the market by involving it in the design and definition of this new idea. He decided to build the pocket transistor radio from the ground up based on what the market wanted. Failure was just an opportunity to learn.

In what has to be one of the most brilliant product rollouts of the twentieth-century consumer electronics industry, Akio Morita allowed the market to shape itself. Over four years TTK transformed itself into Sony and went through four generations of technology until it finally hit the market dead center with its TR-63 in 1957. In the next two years Sony brought out no less than eight additional generations of the pocket transistor radio, each one the embodiment of numerous lessons learned. By then it had sold more than a million pocket transistor radios. The breakthrough pace of Sony's innovating was unprecedented, and it quickly became the hallmark of its agile brand.

Despite the enormous, seemingly unsurpassable success of the pocket transistor radio, the product Sony is perhaps best known for globally is another simple and innocuous device, which it introduced in 1979—the Walkman.

At the time Sony had been struggling with its aging tape recorder division. Competitors such as Panasonic and Olympus were selling a new breed of mini and micro tape cassette recorders. At the other end of the spectrum, large boom boxes had also become very popular. In general, these devices were bellwethers for the personalization of music, which was already in full swing with the abundance of diversity and new genres. But nobody was pulling far enough ahead of the pack. Radios and cassette players were being repackaged every which way to make them more portable. However, they were still not *personal*. Without a truly personal experience the market did not know what to ask for. Yet providers feared venturing too far into the unknown and losing the market they understood.

To innovate, you must be able to mobilize instantly to bring an idea to market and be quickly prepared for failure and reconfiguration. Such was the case at Sony when its tape recorder division stumbled on a refinement to its Pressman personal recorder: Someone got the bright idea to add a simple stereo player and miniature headphones.

*"Markets don't know how to ask for what they haven't yet experienced."*

While it is often difficult for us to recall today what life was once like, try to imagine the shock of being told for the first time that you were going to buy a product that would allow you to go out in public and isolate yourself from your friends and family, or to go out in traffic and to shopping malls without hearing the cars or people within inches of you. The response from Sony's competitors and focus groups was predictable: The idea of a personal player with headphones was just absurd!

Innovation was again the enemy. Nobody sane would go where the fear was.

Morita sensed the green field and jumped on it. Morita's bet was always on the market's appetite for innovation, the sort of innovation that it did not know to ask for. He eschewed focus groups, the opinions of competitors, and even his own marketing team.

Morita's attitude seems cocky, perhaps arrogant, to many, but it reminds me of a conversation I once had with Peter Drucker on the topic of great inventions. I asked Drucker why he thought radical new products, such as the Walkman, always take the market and large incumbents by surprise. "Markets don't know how to ask for what they haven't yet experienced," Drucker told me. Yet, had Morita not been as willing to fail and retry on the market's own terms, his approach surely would have doomed Sony from the start.

But failing fast was important. Early Walkman models were marketed to couples. The Walkman was pitched as a *date experience!* Sony even went so far as to include an emergency cutoff button that would enable a built-in microphone to capture ambient sound so that you could suspend your intimate listening and hear the outside world through your Walkman.

Because of Morita's ability to fail fast and abandon his ideas in favor of the market's, nothing Sony developed ever got stuck as an invention. Instead Sony flooded the market with one innovation after another. It was an endless deluge of innovations, each slightly better than the last, each slightly less expensive, each slightly more in tune with the buyer—call it relentless reinvention through failure.

*Innovation is an unforgiving, constantly accelerating treadmill.*

It's easy to get too wrapped up in the product side of innovation because it's the end result, in Sony's case the Walkman, that's visible, so the object seems to be the innovation. But the object is only the end result of an amazingly integrated and spontaneous organization. Sony was able to innovate not only because of Morita's ethos but because of the processes it had put into place to allow ideas to flourish in a climate of creation. The risk for Sony ultimately was not the risk of new ideas but instead the risk of not having new ideas. Innovation is an unforgiving, constantly accelerating treadmill. Once you jump on you have little choice but to move faster with each step with no graceful way to get off.

Sony had to move on. It needed to move forward and abandon its success once again, and it couldn't do it. Staying in the Innovation Zone is never guaranteed.

## Abandon the Success of the Past: Apple and the iPod

Sony found its way into the Innovation Zone and stayed there for half a century. But staying in the Innovation Zone requires one of the hardest things for any successful person or organization: letting go of the models that define the past.

*Abandoning success isn't about tossing out all previous knowledge. Instead it's about not being bound by the limits of the past in testing the limits of the future.*

The error most of us make is that we move forward as if the ideas and experiments of the past are limited to the variables of the past. But the variables change. In the case of the transistor radio the combination of a new generation of young rock-and-roll fans, the need for radio transmissions to warn citizens in the case of nuclear attack, and the increasing mobility of the population all created a platform and environment of radical change that was ready for portable, battery-powered radio.

Economic variables change, making ideas affordable that were once much too expensive. Growing scale also makes it possible to realize benefit from ideas that start out looking like nothing more than novelties. Think of e-mail, which is only useful if enough people have it. Convenience, security, and demographics are also variables that change the viability of an idea dramatically. So while it is certainly wise to learn the lessons of the past, it is just as important to be able to abandon them when the context of those lessons has changed enough to make a difference.

The problem, of course, is that you can rarely if ever factor in all the external complexities that may constitute an adequate change. This seems like an impossible predicament. It isn't. Abandoning success isn't about tossing out all previous knowledge. Instead it's about not being bound by the limits of the past in testing the limits of the future.

For two decades Sony continued to dominate the market for personal music with its Walkman, through a steady proliferation of models. Yet Sony was not infallible.

The first indications that something was wrong started in 1975 when Sony introduced the Betamax videotape format and began a long battle over both the rights to Betamax and the popularity of the competing VHS standard. Sony got lost in the mistake of trying to invent rather than to innovate, in trying to repair broken dreams rather than create new ones.

In 1989, Akio Morita stepped down as chairman of Sony. In the coming decade Sony's divisions built tall silos, competing with each other as much as the rest of the market, and the company lost its grip on the personal player market it had defined. An outsider made a bet that followed Morita's pattern of innovation so closely and so predictably that its eclipse of Sony is nothing short of poetic irony. This new company's innovation was built on the market that Sony and many of its competitors had created with personalization, digital music, and miniaturization. The company was, of course, Apple Computer, and the innovation is the now legendary iPod.

In the same way that Sony's TR-63 was not the first transistor radio, the iPod was not the first MP3 player, not by a long shot. In fact it was not the least expensive, nor was it the smallest, nor by any measure the incumbent. In fact, Apple was the outsider in the music business. Apple no more created the popular MP3 format, which all iPod music used, than Sony had created the transistor. But Apple created the experience by bringing together the interface, digital media, and the ability to buy music at its most atomic level and create truly personalized playlists. And, most important, it let the market run with it.

Apple's approach was seen as the enemy to established players. The person who led iPod development was Tony Fadell, who had actually approached all the market's incumbents with his idea of creating a device that would benefit from the use of a high-capacity hard disk and an online music store where users could purchase music rather than subscribe to it. The incumbents turned Fadell away at the doorstep. Doing it Fadell's way would undermine the established model and require walking away from success, fighting with incumbents who owned the content, and confusing the market with an approach that was not the norm.

Fadell finally found an unlikely welcome at Apple, which had years before sworn off consumer electronics with its own failed efforts at PDAs and the very visible disaster of its Newton. Within just eight months, Fadell and his team had developed the first iPod prototype, built on PortalPlayer, a software technology Apple acquired from another company! Fadell refined PortalPlayer, combined it with components from the now discontinued Newton, added navigation controls radically different from the Walkman's (which were painfully inept at managing a large music collection), and included the Apple iTunes Music Store along with synchronization software to link it to a user's desktop.

Apple had the benefit of understanding the critical role of experience. Apple's core competency had always been the crucial interface between mind and machine. It understood how machines and people worked together best, and could rapidly zero in on the essential elements of experience. Apple also understood the value of intimacy in a customer relationship. Historically, Apple has had a strong cult following based on a sense its users have that it really understands the way they behave. Within a few months of the launch, the future of the iPod was clear. By the time this book is released Apple will have sold more than one hundred million iPods, and iPod users will have downloaded more than two billion songs. Nearly half of all music purchased will be purchased in digital form over the Internet. People will look back and wonder how they possibly lived without iTunes and portable digital music libraries. Behavior will be altered so dramatically that both consumers and producers will be convinced that nothing could take the iPod's place, and with that the door to the next innovation will crack open.

## Separate the Seeds from the Weeds: General Motors and OnStar

Sony and Apple illustrate the way innovation can be limited by the notion of how things have been done, how businesses have worked, and what consumers have expected. Innovation doesn't work by building on expectations. It creates ecosystems where unknown seeds and plants will eventually thrive. The job of innovative organizations is as much to keep a careful eye out for new growth as to tend to the seeds originally planted.

*In established industries the seeds of change can act more like irritants.*

That's an incredibly difficult thing to do in larger organizations where the culture has been built around a legacy of operational excellence and business models that rest on extensive supply chains and well-established procedures for production. Few industries come as close to that sort of established legacy business model as does the automotive industry, which is steeped in a century of practices and attitudes.

Even with the influence of Japan's automobile industry, the fundamental business of selling automobiles has barely changed since its inception. Yet even here innovation can have a radical impact in reshaping the attitudes and models of the business. What if we were to rethink the automobile industry of the future? What might it look like? Would manufacturing automobiles still be part of that business model? Now imagine planting the seeds for that sort of change.

In established industries the seeds of change can act more like irritants that threaten to bring the well-lubricated wheels of progress to a grinding halt. In these environments separating the seeds from the weeds rests on having a committed leader and an Innovation Zone where new ideas can be protected as they take shape.

## PLANTING THE SEEDS OF CHANGE

In 1995 Project Beacon, a partnership of GM's Hughes Electronics, EDS, and GM's car business, was an uncertain venture with no clear path forward. Yet, Harry Pearce, GM's retired vice chairman, saw in Project Beacon a glimpse of the future in which mobile communications and the automobile could be brought together. Pearce selected longtime GM middle manager Chet Huber to head the project. Huber was an engineer with a Harvard MBA and a degree from the Industrial College of the Armed Forces, all of which would be essential as he spent the next six months looking at how GM could build a business around the Project Beacon portfolio. The portfolio included the nascent technology of GPS, a tiny opportunity that at the time could only generously be called a seed within the enormity of the automobile industry, where new innovations are measured by their contributions in billions of dollars. In this context it just wasn't clear what the payoff from combining mobile communications, GPS, and automobiles would be.

The bigger challenge in doing anything new in the automotive industry, however, was to break open the vehicle development process and make it fast enough to accommodate the pace needed for smaller-scale innovations. GM couldn't introduce an innovation of any magnitude in the time it took to integrate new technology into an automobile. According to Chet, "If we had to live by the traditional rules of engagement for vehicle programs, then from the concept to our first application would have been three or four years." That was just too long.

The first step was creating an Innovation Zone—a new business called General Motors Mobile Communications Services that acted as a demilitarized zone between Hughes, EDS, and GM. This provided the neutrality that the new idea needed to be unencumbered by past legacy and culture and to survive long enough to determine its value.

The idea quickly formed to build a device that would enhance vehicle safety by using positioning and telemetry to report accidents, unlock doors, and locate stolen vehicles. Some basic market research was done to validate the interest in a device that might increase the safety of automobiles using GPS; the initial feedback was encouraging, although far from definitive.

High-level support for the project was crucial, and fortunately it was there from the beginning. In addition to Pearce, Rick Wagoner, forty-one-year-old general manager of GM North America, was fully behind the idea. Chet and Rick met informally once a month for several months to cultivate the new service, now called OnStar, and to integrate it into GM's culture. Huber recalls that they agreed, "If you cannot suspend the rules of nature on the vehicle development side we should not even start, because we are going to end up embarrassing everybody. We will end up with a business model that does not work because the technology will be old by definition as soon as we start and we'll end up with just cycles of frustration."

*Leadership has to accept the responsibility of creating a protected space in which new ideas can thrive long enough to prove their value.*

It was no small task. It soon became apparent that Huber's challenge was about more than simply integrating OnStar with automobile manufacturing; it was about stretching GM to a new level of innovation. GM had to challenge itself to do something that was going to cause discomfort in GM's core business model in a mature market with a lot of competitive intensity and excess capacity. This is the fundamental insight I've observed in every organization that manages to extend itself into new markets through innovation. Leadership has to accept the responsibility of creating a protected space in which new ideas can thrive long enough to prove their value.

To do this Huber and Wagoner agreed to create a new GM division, with Huber at the helm.

In November 1995 the OnStar Division went to work. By September 1996 Chet and his people were ready to go to market, an amazing feat in itself in the automobile industry, where it should have taken at least three times as long. The processes stretched GM to its limits and, in Chet's own words, "tested every aspect of GM's sense of humor." But it also proved that GM was fully capable of radical innovation.

In the two years after its introduction OnStar garnered only a thousand subscribers. But within ten years it had four million. Today an amazing 93–94 percent of all GM vehicles include OnStar, and it's nearing the milestone of one hundred million service interactions in total since its inception. In addition, the OnStar brand is one of the most recognized in the United States. OnStar has been used by other auto manufacturers, and its expansion into the Chinese market has recently been announced. The technology has nearly four hundred patent applications to back it, and a new patent is being filed every seven days!

Interestingly, the most significant innovation is not the product itself. It's the relationship OnStar has created between GM and its customers.

OnStar is one of the first and most effective ways to link GM to its customers on an ongoing basis. For instance, OnStar can automatically assess a vehicle's key operating systems diagnostic and send a monthly e-mail to the owner. Sounds good, but at first dealers were up in arms. Many customers would postpone their dealer notice to get an oil change every three thousand miles, waiting for the OnStar e-mail to tell them when the oil needed to be changed based on GM's oil-life monitoring systems. Dealers soon saw that OnStar actually led to even greater value when owners came in for repairs with a complete printout of all the diagnostics OnStar had performed. Not only did this uncover issues before they became problems but it also increased the perceived reliability of the vehicle. In many cases the fact that the diagnostic came back with a clean bill of health was as important to reinforcing the brand as it was to the service that was needed. This is a far cry from how the service was envisioned when it was first deployed and safety was the entirety of the value proposition.

*Creating an Innovation Zone has deep impact not just in terms of the product being created but the fundamental changes to the business as well.*

Although OnStar began as a safety device, today OnStar receives nearly four unlock calls (requests to unlock a member's car when the keys are locked in) and thirty route support calls for directions for every safety request that comes in.

With five million people using OnStar and five thousand new subscriptions each day, OnStar has become the strongest customer relationship program in the automotive industry—building that sort of relationship with customers by itself would have cost GM as much if not more than developing the OnStar technology and service has!

The net result has been to shift GM from being just a vehicle manufacturer to a relationship manager with a direct connection to and from the customer. This is the essence of creating an Innovation Zone that has deep impact not just in terms of the product being created but the fundamental changes to the business as well. The wonderful thing about innovation of this sort is that it spurs new innovations, not only within the organization but across an industry. The seed turns into a flourishing ecosystem, and each change spurs myriad others.

For example, as automobile manufacturers have become much more safety conscious, the devices used to protect passengers during an accident—air bags, air curtains, reinforced interiors, frames with crumple zones, and so on—result in significantly reduced external bruising. However, doctors rely on these telltale marks to help them identify internal injuries, which are an especially prevalent result of side impacts. Ironically, without those telltales, they lose the ability to quickly diagnose the location and severity of an injury. To address this problem, OnStar has developed Advanced Crash Response, which provides a digital crash signature detailing the many dimensions of a collision, such as impact force, direction of impact, and whether or not a rollover has occurred. OnStar is working with the National Highway Traffic Safety Administration and the CDC to create algorithms to interpret the digital crash signatures so that they can be meaningfully and easily used by the six thousand 911 jurisdictions across the country to respond better to crash scenes. Estimates are that this information can increase survivability of an impact by more than 25 percent.

In addition, systems are being considered for advanced auto crash notification that will send data about a crash to the emergency room prior to the crash victim's arrival to determine which specialists are needed and which facilities are best suited to deal with the possible injuries. OnStar has also rolled out a service used in conjunction with law enforcement to not only locate but actually slow a vehicle down safely and bring it to a stop when it is being chased by police.

Where might OnStar go from here? That's the wrong question. A better question might be, Where will the automotive industry, especially the U.S. automotive industry, go from here as the result of OnStar? The possible answers make it clear that innovation is much more about changing a business than about delivering any single product or service.

## Focus on Process over Product: 3M and Post-it Notes

Few companies have the reputation of 3M when it comes to innovation. Founded in 1902, the 3M brand symbolizes a century of bringing ideas to market across a diverse range of industries including adhesives, abrasives, pharmaceuticals, fabrics, film, coatings, and reprographics. Amazingly, despite fifty thousand products over a hundred years, most people today know 3M best for one product: the Post-it Note.

At the heart of 3M's history of innovation is a strong culture of taking risk and supporting a cultural commitment to the process of innovation. From the company's first products, the founders instilled a spirit of experimentation and resiliency in the face of daunting odds. When 3M's very first product, an abrasive for grinding wheels, faltered due to poor raw materials, the company turned to making sandpaper—something the founders knew virtually nothing about! But the sandpaper the company produced was widely criticized by customers. According to 3M's customers, the abrasive just fell off the sandpaper when it was used. A 3M employee working in the company's plant noticed that waste abrasive that had been discarded into a bucket of water had an oily residue. As it turned out, the abrasive had come from the supplier by ship along with a cargo of olive oil that broke open during the voyage and mixed with the garnet abrasive, making the garnet impossible to glue permanently to the sandpaper! Undeterred, 3M researchers found a way to cook the oil off the garnet. Such was the humble start of an innovation powerhouse.

*From 3M's first products, the founders instilled a spirit of experimentation and resiliency.*

One of the cornerstones of 3M's innovation culture is what has been called the 15 percent rule. Simply put, the 15 percent rule states that every technical employee at 3M can spend up to 15 percent of the time working on independent projects. The rule had its origins in the early days of 3M when an enterprising young engineer began to devote time to the problem of tape used in painting cars. At the time two-tone car bodies was starting to become a popular trend. However, the plaster tape used by painters would either peel away the paint or leave a residue on the surface. In either case the result was hours of additional prep. A 3M employee who was responsible for providing 3M's WetDry sandpaper to body shops noticed this and began to research adhesives that could handle the challenge. In 1925 3M introduced masking tape. Five years later that research led to the introduction of cellophane tape.

This approach has continued as a cornerstone of 3M's innovation philosophy to this day. A 3M executive told me that the philosophy at 3M is to reward not only successful innovation but failed attempts as well. This sounds absurd but it is at the heart of 3M's success with Post-it Notes.

The adhesive used in Post-it Notes was developed with no specific application in mind. According to its creator, Spencer Silver, "My discovery was a solution waiting for a problem to solve." Spencer's collaborator Art Fry (often credited with the idea of applying Silver's adhesive to paper) says, "At 3M we're a bunch of ideas. We never throw an idea away because you never know when someone else may need it."

This would sound like a very inefficient way to go about innovation were it not for the fact that it comes from one of the world's most successful and consistently innovative companies, one that, according to internal documents, averages a whopping 30 percent of sales from products less than four years old. That sort of track record is hard to argue with. But it's also incredibly difficult to sustain, especially for a $20 billion company.

*Sustained innovation without a well-grounded process is simply not possible in large-scale organizations.*

In 2002 3M decided it needed to turn more attention to the fuzzy front end of innovation by evaluating ways to increase the flow of new ideas and evaluate them across the organization's many research and product groups.

The company needed to figure out a way to provide visibility to new ideas. The solution was an automated innovation management platform that served as a place for ideas to be submitted, inventoried, evaluated, and connected to problems. It was the place for solutions that were still waiting for problems— among which 3M can hope for the next Post-it Note.

Ideas saw a large increase during the initial implementation, with forty-two coming in during the first thirty days. Eighteen of the first fifty-four submissions (33 percent) became qualified—almost triple the industry standard.

According to 3M, the quantity of ideas increased tenfold within just ninety days of deploying an innovation management system. Once again, at 3M as with many other large companies, scale and speed of innovation will almost always demand a sophisticated process to manage ideas. It's one thing to have a cultural foundation for innovation, but this alone may not be enough as your organization grows and demands more coordination of ideas across large regions and disciplines. Sustained innovation without a well-grounded process is simply not possible in large-scale organizations.

## Create an Innovation Experience: Cheskin

We take for granted today that all companies are driven by the need to innovate and that all buyers expect innovation. But it wasn't always that way. While the value of innovation may have always been part of the move toward new products and services, we often forget how recent the notion of continuous innovation is.

For example, in 1900 the average duration of a monopoly (the average time for a new competitive entry to establish a threat to the incumbent) was nearly forty years. In that climate innovation happened across the span of decades. By 1940 that time period had dropped to less than ten years. By the turn of the twenty-first century it was less than twelve months.[1] Simply put, this means that, as consumers, we have not only come to expect constant innovation but we will not settle for less. Innovation has become table stakes for all industries and products. The problem, both for companies delivering innovation and markets consuming it, is that our focus is still on the innovation of the product.

For the better part of the twentieth century the value of innovation resided entirely in the product. But there comes a point when you hit a hard stop in how fast you can change a product. You can only retool a factory so fast. Quality control, skills, manufacturing processes, partnerships, and supply chains all need time to be built, reconfigured, and synchronized. No matter how agile you are, there are limits to change; even in a service industry the same basic principle applies. So how do you continue to accelerate innovation beyond these apparently immutable bounds?

To answer that question, stop and think of an innovative company. Whatever company you came up with has probably added value to your life by providing much more than just a product—it has also changed the way you experience some aspect of the world. This notion of experience is at the heart of the shift in innovation from just products to services. Consider many of the companies that have innovated in mature markets—Wal-Mart in retail, JetBlue in air transport, Home Depot in hardware, Zipcar in urban car rental, even Apple in entertainment. What you think of most when these companies come to mind is the experience of using their service.

You can continue to accelerate innovation, and the value it delivers, by shifting the focus from product innovation to experience innovation. Unlike products, experiences can be innovated in infinitely variable ways and in many cases directly by the user through the use of personalization. Experience is also the most profound source of value from any product or service. When you think about the brands you find to be the most valuable and important in your life, it is likely that you associate them with a meaningful experience.

*You can continue to accelerate innovation, and the value it delivers, by shifting the focus from product innovation to experience innovation.*

This may seem like we are slicing the onion a bit thin. After all, what's the difference between a product and an experience? For companies like Apple, the product and the experience seem to be tightly intertwined. Consider the iPod. Is it a product or an experience? You can certainly see it, hold it, feel it, and, of course, hear it. But could the iPod exist without the iTunes store? Would it be anywhere near as popular without the connection it has both in terms of the experience of using it and the experience of belonging to a community of devotees who also use it? Likely not. Innovating experience requires a conscious effort to understand not just how people use a product but also to understand why they use it.

## CONNECTING INNOVATION TO EXPERIENCE

Understanding this intimate connection between innovation and experience is one of the most important lessons to learn in moving any organization toward higher levels of innovation and value. However, this is not a new idea. The history and science of understanding the influence of experience on innovation goes back at least seventy years, well before the iPod, and it has affected nearly every aspect of our lives.

In the 1930s Louis Cheskin and his company, which evolved to become Cheskin Added Value, embarked on one of the most radical efforts to understand consumer buying behaviors and to answer the question, Why do consumers buy? Cheskin's work shaped of some of the world's most prominent and iconic brands, including Marlboro, Tide, Crest, Dove, McDonald's, Standard Oil, 3M, Lifesavers, Atari, and Betty Crocker. It's difficult to find anyone today who does not interact daily with one of the brands that Cheskin touched. Cheskin's ability to understand the way markets behave was founded on a deep conviction that people develop an association with the image of a brand and the statement it makes.

In the 1930s and 1940s the notion that a brand could convey value, much less innovation, was a novel idea. But at the same time there was an explosion of several fundamental trends that created an innovation apex for Cheskin. These included the advent of mass markets, mass distribution systems, mass transportation, mass media, and economies of scale that caused every company to look for ways to sell more by inventing new product categories. Innovation in this era was steeped in product and invention. The explosion of new ideas, products, and markets created choices, but it also created confusion.

To differentiate themselves, companies started moving slowly toward the more effuse notion of a brand as a way to make their product experience unique. The products Cheskin consulted on were in many cases commodities, so the move was essential. Products such as soap, cigarettes, and fast food used the same basic ingredients and processes, yet they were still able to create a strong brand attraction and loyalty. Cheskin's approach was to identify the fundamental drivers of buyers in order to present the product in a way that best fit their perception of value. Sometimes this was a subtle exercise, as when he suggested changing the color of margarine from white to yellow, dramatically increasing demand for margarine and setting the stage for every other margarine since.

This attachment to brand became a defining factor in marketing but it also led to a fair amount of disillusionment as companies began to develop an "if we build it they will come" attitude. Recall, for example, Sony and its failed efforts to capture the MP3 market. Companies in that era felt that once a brand was established they had a lock on the market. Cheskin realized that the market's perception of value had to be understood and leveraged to create an experience that was in keeping with the market's future direction.

*Value and, by asso-
ciation, innovation
exist entirely in the
experience of the
customer.*

Cheskin was incredibly astute in this regard. In one of his most famous examples he lambasted Ford's plans to release the Edsel in 1957. He believed that the Edsel lacked the modernism that the market expected of an automobile. Instead he praised the Ford Thunderbird. Ford and his contemporaries denounced Cheskin but not for long. Shortly after both the Edsel and the Thunderbird had made their mark, through the respective failure and success that Cheskin had predicted, Ford retained Cheskin to help design and market both the Mustang and the Lincoln Continental, two of Ford's most successful cars. For the Lincoln Continental, Cheskin actually recommended incorporating design elements from the recently launched Sputnik satellite and promoting the car through a series of experience-based events at high-profile locations where elite drivers would congregate.

What Cheskin did in these cases was to integrate experience with product. But wait, isn't that the equivalent of slapping "new and improved" on the packaging? Absolutely not. Cheskin understood that invention alone was not enough. The Edsel was full of new technology and gadgets, including a first-of-its-kind push-button transmission! But this oddity did not create an experience that was valuable to the consumer. The experience of the Edsel was steeped in imagery that outdated it before it rolled off the assembly line. It's a great example of one of the five laws of innovation: Innovation is not invention. Just because you can create something new, technically amazing, and unique does not mean it has value in the eyes of the market. Value and, by association, innovation exist entirely in the experience of the customer.

## THE MEANING OF INNOVATION

Louis Cheskin's ideas and philosophy are as relevant today as they were in 1957. Darrel Rhea, current CEO of the company Cheskin founded, takes this notion of experience-based innovation one step further. He believes that those companies that are best positioned to lead the market through innovation are the ones that create deep meaning in the experience of using their products or services.

In their book *Making Meaning: How Successful Businesses Deliver Meaningful Customer Experiences,*[2] coauthors Steve Diller, Nathan Shedroff, and Darrel Rhea lay out the premise that innovation is not just about creating or managing experiences or even having novel and differentiating experiences. Instead it's about creating what they call *meaningful* experiences. According to the authors, meaningful experiences are those that make life worth living by connecting and expressing our values as human beings.

They have taken this idea and created something akin to a Maslovian hierarchy of innovation experiences. They explain that at the lowest level of the hierarchy we can have an economic experience. This is an experience where we get a product for a good price. This defines the commodity world, where products are the same in quality and function and differ only in price. At the next level we can have a functional experience, which means that a product really suits our needs and performs the job we expect it to do. If we get both a good economic experience and a good functional experience, our perceived value increases by an order of magnitude. Beyond that we can have an emotional experience with a product, which is to say that we get some kind of visceral response from interacting with the product, something we'll typically pay a premium for.

Diller, Shedroff, and Rhea assert that a higher level of value can be provided by a status or identity experience. Such experiences make us feel good about what the product or service says about who we are to other people. Think of luxury or designer items. Many people will pay a lot more for a T-shirt with a polo player on it or luggage with an *LV* monogram because it says something about themselves to their peers. On the other hand, some of us will pay more for a socially responsible brand, such as a bottle of water from Ethos, whose mission it is to help children around the world get clean water. In each case the product innovation is that it enhances the meaning of the experience and adds value that we would not otherwise get from the product alone.

*Stylistic change barely passes for innovation but it has become prevalent as companies try to keep up with the expectation to innovate. It's easy and it's cheap. But it doesn't deliver a new or more meaningful experience.*

This leads to the highest level of value in the authors' model, the meaningful experience, which reinforces the value of our lives. As Rhea told me in a 2008 interview: "Companies need to focus their innovation not just on providing functional and economic benefits. People have plenty of stuff; what we want as human beings are products we love. People want products that reflect who they are as people—products that cause us to say, 'This is a product that was made just for me; whoever designed this really gets who I am;

this is made by a company that knows who I want to be.'" This phenomenon dramatically alters the nature of innovation from the creation of product to a collaborative exercise between provider and consumer in the creation of personalized value.

However, the challenge for many companies is that in their intuitive attempt to articulate what's missing in their products, they often fall back on simply redesigning them, which in its worst form gets translated into just another style. For example, "Don't buy water in bottles shaped like bottles—buy our water in bottles shaped like pears." This sort of stylistic change barely passes for innovation but it has become prevalent as companies try to keep up with the market expectation to innovate. It's easy and it's cheap. But it doesn't deliver a new or more meaningful experience. It is the equivalent of putting a Ferrari body on the chassis, engine, drive train, and interior of a Honda Civic (we'll assume we could make the two fit together). I'm not putting down Honda Civics, which have their own cult following and sense of meaning, but if I'm buying a Ferrari, I want the experience of a Ferrari, and that won't come just from a red car shaped like a wedge.

This sort of innovation illusionism ultimately backfires. The problem is that companies who simply follow style have separated the innovation promise of their brand from the innovation of the experience. They are pursuing what people buy, not why they buy. In many cases these companies have created different silos for each, with one group of people looking at and creating what the brand promise of innovation is and trying to attract more customers, while another group, in a separate silo, is producing the product. This is the classic problem, described earlier, of how innovation is limited to one confined area of most organizations.

The authors' point, which I think is the essential ingredient missing in many attempts to innovate, is that organizations need to think about how to innovate the customer experience first by asking, "Why do customers buy?" and then work backward to integrate the various components of the organization needed to deliver that experience. The bottom line is that the innovation experience promised by the brand cannot be separate from the innovation of the product. Examples of companies that do this well can be found in all industries, from the Ritz and Kimpton hotels, to Lexus and BMW, to Apple and Research in Motion (developers of the BlackBerry personal digital assistant), to eBay and Amazon.com. In each case the brand and the product move in lockstep to deliver an experience that extends far beyond the product to the much deeper connection with the user. These companies are the ones that get the highest grades for innovation and the value of their innovations. They are companies that keep their promise to the market to build meaningful experiences.

## FEEDING GOLIATH

A final consideration in moving toward an innovation experience is that today's businesses are huge compared to what they used to be. The challenge for these monolithic companies is to maintain a level of growth that satisfies their investor community. It's infinitely easier to take a company from $10 million in revenues to $50 million than it is to take one from $1 billion to $5 billion.

These large companies have been forced to increase earnings and growth through cost cutting, operational efficiencies, mergers, and acquisitions. This works up to a point but it also represents a tumultuous mix of change with a good dose of risk. In large companies cutting costs inevitably leads to a limited appetite for innovation. Mergers and acquisitions (M&A) are also enormously challenging from a cultural standpoint, especially when a large company acquires a smaller, more innovative company. The culture clash can quickly squash the great ideas that created the value that was acquired.

*Google's innovations may be supported by targeted acquisitions, but it is important to note that the innovations are not driven by the acquisition.*

This is why the market rewards companies that can grow primarily through organic innovation. This does not mean that these companies cannot also engage in M&A but rather that they are not bound to growth only through M&A. One of the best current examples is Google, the Internet search giant that has transformed the Internet experience for the vast majority of us through its constant stream of innovations.

Google's innovations may be supported by targeted acquisitions, but it is important to note that the innovations are not driven by the acquisition. Take, for example, Google's purchase of YouTube for $1.6 billion. At the time Google already had in place the same functionality to host and share video. However, it lacked the user experience and community that YouTube had created. What's interesting about the history of the acquisition is that it was widely criticized at the time due to the fact that Google was buying technology that it already had built on its own. But this only points out how deeply engrained the notion of product is for most of us. Google was not buying a product; it was buying a way to round out the Google experience for its users. By keeping the YouTube brand separate but connecting it to the experience of Google, it created a fundamental innovation in its market without building a product.

Most companies lose sight of this distinction between product and experience. They are great at leveraging operational efficiencies but are usually not well regarded as innovators, and when they do acquire companies that are great innovators, they soon pummel the innovation out of them, leading to a declining level of performance over time.

As the marketplace and investors increasingly put pressure on companies to answer the fundamental question "What are you doing about innovation?" we will no doubt see more attention being paid to the topic of innovation. Much of that will end up in the category of old wine in new bottles. But this is just the background noise of companies who have yet to understand the value and the meaning of experience in innovation. Those companies that do pull ahead will focus on ways to innovate both the products and the experiences of their customers by focusing not just on what markets want but why they want it.

## Challenge Conventional Wisdom: The iRobot Story

Few things have captured our image of the future better than the twentieth-century icon of innovation, the robot. Czechoslovakian playwright Karel Capek first introduced the word in his play *Rossum's Universal Robots,* but it was Isaac Asimov who popularized it in his short story "Runaround," where he first defined the "three laws of robotics."

Since then the robot has been idealized in thousands of books, movies, and television shows, from *The Jetsons* to *Lost in Space* and from R2D2 to Wall-e. The robot has become the constant companion of the future, promising to make our lives easier by performing household chores and serving us tirelessly.

Those of us who grew up with this image of the mechanical servant never had any doubt that at some point robots would indeed be common household companions. But we also quickly came to the conclusion that the future was further out than anyone expected. For most of us robots would never be more than a novelty gadget. And a litany of consumer robots including Sony's AIBO robotic dog, Honda's Asimo, LEGO's Mindstorms, and the ever-popular Robosapian humanoid toy robots conditioned us to expect very little from consumer robots beyond an expensive toy that even the most ardent enthusiasts quickly tired of.

At the same time that our mechanical friend was being popularized in early media, Marvin Minsky was establishing the first artificial intelligence lab at the Massachusetts Institute of Technology. Minsky's early work set the stage for fifty years of robotics, leading to a tremendous surge of investment and application of robots in manufacturing. Yet robots in the home were still an elusive dream. That is, until iRobot came along.

In the 1980s Colin Angle was a graduate student at MIT. He was fascinated by robotics and was working on developing a six-legged mechanical version. Angle's project ended up as the basis for his master's thesis. However, after working painstakingly to develop his robot, Angle had a hollow feeling. It dawned on him that, despite its technical prowess, his six-legged marvel was nothing more than a curiosity, an odd but interesting techno-toy. The realization dawned on him that there was no value there, just cool technology. This was not an innovation as much as it was just one more link in a long chain of interesting but otherwise useless inventions.

That was a turning point for Angle. He quickly decided to turn his focus to creating value through robots rather than just chasing after technology. In 1990 he was joined by cofounder Helen Greiner and Rodney Brooks and created a new company, iRobot. The mission for iRobot was simple and straightforward: "Build cool stuff, deliver great product, make money, have fun, and change the world."

iRobot made a mark for itself by building robots for extraterrestrial exploration, military use on battlefields and minefields, and in 2001 searching the rubble of the World Trade Center in the aftermath of the terrorist attack. The company grew steadily, but the consumer market was still elusive. Colin Angle thought it was time to take a crack at the consumer once again, but this time without the hyperbole and promise of a robot maid-of-all-work. He took a much more practical approach.

Angle entered a 150-year-old industry where extensive innovation had already occurred. Yet an innovation apex was approaching and the timing for his idea couldn't have been better. While much of the tedium of housework has been automated to operate in parallel mode—that is, your dishwasher, washing machine, and oven can all work simultaneously, without your constant attention—one aspect of keeping a house clean has barely progressed since the early part of the last century: cleaning your floors. Vacuuming and mopping have experienced countless incremental innovations but still require someone to attend to the entire task. At the same time the importance of this simple task has increased in response to airborne pollutants, respiratory conditions such as asthma, the growing footprint of the typical home, and the premium placed on time in two-income households.

Suddenly you have several substantial catalysts that change the nature of the problem significantly. If you build vacuum cleaners and floor mops, how do you respond to these issues? Well, of course, you make the tool faster, cleaner, lighter, stronger—whatever is needed to make the task easier. Your focus is on *the task,* and that doesn't allow you to ask if the task even needs to be done. Companies that challenge conventional wisdom don't start by asking, "How can we make this task easier?" They start by asking, "Do we need this task at all?"

So assume that your company sells vacuum cleaners and I suggest that the problem is the task itself and we should eliminate the need to do the task. It wouldn't take long for you to show me the door. But this is exactly the situation that an innovation apex creates and the way iRobot challenged conventional wisdom.

In 2002 iRobot introduced the Roomba, a vacuuming robot that looked nothing like the prototypical sci-fi robot. The idea of a robotic vacuum cleaner wasn't especially inventive. The basic sensors, components, and software had all been developed by iRobot or elsewhere in the robotics industry in some form. According to Angle, for iRobot's thirteen-year history prior to its introduction of the Roomba, friends and associates would consistently ask if iRobot could create a robot to help clean their homes. What stopped iRobot and so many other potential manufacturers, especially the classic incumbent players such as Electrolux, Hoover, and Oreck, from introducing a robot vacuum? Like so many innovations the idea had been set aside as unlikely given the history of consumer robots. Lots of people were willing to buy a traditional vacuum cleaner. In fact, the market itself was very healthy given the catalysts bearing on it.

However, Angle and his colleagues had several things going for them. They were not afraid to experiment; they had a deep core competency in small, compact, low-cost robots from their years of experience in practical solutions for space and military use; and most important, even though they were robot makers, they were not tied to the old notion of a home robot, and they certainly were not tied to the notion of a traditional vacuum cleaner. Angle had learned from his days at MIT that the key was not in the notion of what a robot was but rather in what it could do. In fact the original Roomba packaging did not have a single mention of the word robot (except for the company name). The intent was to keep it simple, practical, and useful.

The small round Roomba disk wasn't expected to sell fifteen thousand units in its first year, and it didn't. It sold more than ninety thousand units! From the outset it was clear that the Roomba had hit a vein of unexploited market demand. Given the option of not vacuuming, people jumped at the opportunity.

The lessons learned from iRobot's success come down to some simple themes that are echoed in many of the Innovation Zone cases I've already talked about. iRobot understood its core competency and played directly to it without getting stuck in a product. The company pursued value rather than technology. The Roomba is simple and effective.

Most important, Angle and his cofounders did not get trapped in the conventional notion of what a robot or a vacuum cleaner was supposed to be, but instead challenged the conventional wisdom of both robotics and the cleaning industry by focusing on what it should do.

## There's No Going Back

The stories about NASA, Apple, Sony, OnStar, 3M, Cheskin, iRobot, and so many others involved in the active process of sustaining innovation share a common and uncannily consistent underlying theme. *Markets have a voice, but they cannot express needs for what they have not yet experienced.* When an innovation like the Walkman or the iPod takes hold and races through the market like a firestorm, we inevitably look back and ask how we could have missed the need and the perfect fit. Yet what we fail to recognize is that markets do not shape innovation as much as they are shaped by it. Profound innovations change the behavior of a market and stretch it so that it can never regain its original form. It's the reason my children look at the old Smith Corona manual typewriter in my library in amazement and disbelief, asking, "How could you possibly have used that?" Their shock is not just at the laborious manual process of typing but even more at the process of thinking without the aid of a computer. Even I wonder how I once was able to compose thoughts without the benefit of a computer.

*Innovators are the eyes and ears of the market when it cannot see and hear.*

Great innovators and organizations understand that this pattern repeats itself, with an infinity of cases and examples yet to be experienced. They accept that their role is to be the eyes and ears of the market when it cannot see and hear. They take responsibility for going where the fear is and taking us all to a new destination, one that was never even on our map—terra incognita, where the edge of the world drops us off its flat surface and into some great unknown.

Great innovation, it would seem, like Michelangelo's *David,* has to be liberated from its confines. It is why innovation seems to run backward in time, bringing us face to face with ideas that appear uncannily familiar once we embrace them. We accept innovation as though it were always meant to be there, even though, like the untrained sculptor, we would never have known to look for it.

## Innovation Recap

Each of the seven lessons of innovation illustrates a specific behavior that is common among innovative companies:

- Build for the unknown.

- Fail fast.

- Abandon the success of the past.

- Separate the seeds from the weeds.

- Focus on process over product.

- Create an innovation experience.

- Challenge conventional wisdom.

CHAPTER 7

# MEASUREMENT AND TECHNOLOGY IN INNOVATION

*People sometimes try to measure innovation by tracking the success of new products. Unfortunately, paying too much attention to that success can quickly derail additional innovation in new products, services, and processes, creating the illusion that protecting the current offering is more important than developing new processes and ideas likely to threaten the product being measured. And every single one of your competitors is constantly devising ways to threaten your current offering; the only way to beat them to it is to play in the same game, however risky it appears.*

The question for anyone serious about investing in innovation becomes, How do we measure the ability to innovate and the success of innovation?

## Measuring Innovation

First, investing in innovation begins when leadership forms a resolute and committed intent to invest in innovation. I have yet to find a single case where an organization in the Innovation Zone was not led by a CEO who believed strongly that innovation is both valuable and measurable. By the same token I've seen many an organization that once was innovative succumb to inertia during the tenure of a CEO who only paid lip service to innovation but did not have a deep belief in its measurable value.

Second, it is possible to assess where your organization ranks in terms of its innovative capacity. Refer to the appendix for a compressed version of the assessment I have used with hundreds of organizations to determine their capability to innovate. It will give you a relative assessment of where your organization ranks in terms of its innovative capacity. A full innovation assessment spans a variety of areas that determine how your organization's practices, behaviors, and attitudes support a culture of innovation. The version in the appendix looks at some of the key indicators of innovation, which are sufficient to provide a basic sense for your organization's ability to create an Innovation Zone.

## Measuring Velocity Through the Innovation Chain

The velocity of innovation in an organization can be measured in very concrete terms and improved by focusing on what I refer to as the *innovation chain* (see Figure 8). Velocity of innovation can be compared and contrasted to competitors' and peer groups' velocity through a simple formula. Four stages determine the velocity of an innovation chain:

- Internal awareness
- Internal responsiveness
- External responsiveness
- External awareness

### INTERNAL AWARENESS

In its simplest terms, internal awareness is the ability of an organization to quickly assess its inventory of skills and core competencies. This appears to be a simple task, yet few organizations have mastered it.

Innovative organizations ask "What do we do?" rather than "What do we make?" For example, it's easy to say that a residential architect designs ranch-style houses or split-levels. But what happens to the architect if demand for these types of buildings declines or even disap-

FIGURE 8. **THE INNOVATION CHAIN**

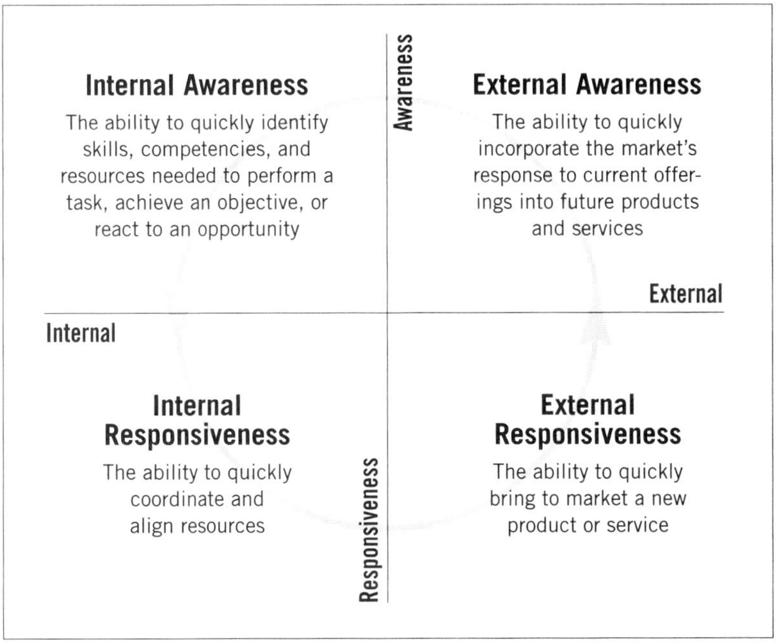

| **Internal Awareness** Awareness | **External Awareness** |
|---|---|
| The ability to quickly identify skills, competencies, and resources needed to perform a task, achieve an objective, or react to an opportunity | The ability to quickly incorporate the market's response to current offerings into future products and services |

Internal

External

| **Internal Responsiveness** | **External Responsiveness** |
|---|---|
| The ability to quickly coordinate and align resources   Responsiveness | The ability to quickly bring to market a new product or service |

*The innovation chain measures how quickly and effectively your organization can innovate.*

pears? Competencies refer to deeply rooted processes for understanding and adding value, and they always outlive products and services.

Strong emphasis on the functional organization structures and hierarchies that often permeate traditional companies inhibits the development of internal awareness. Organizations with a rigid functional structure most often define their core competency in terms of their products and services, not their skills.

It is this long-term emphasis on skills that organizations need most if they are to weather changing markets. But the systems and institutions in place in many organizations undermine this objective.

Good ideas meet plenty of obstacles en route to senior management's agenda. In a global study conducted recently by the Delphi Group, fully half of the three hundred corporate professionals polled indicated that where they work, a good idea is easily stunted by bureaucracy, is often abandoned by its creator, or has a better chance of finding success outside the organization rather than within

*Innovative organizations ask "What do we do?" rather than "What do we make?"*

it. Anecdotal evidence abounds, too: It is easy for most of us to list the obstacles we have faced in getting our ideas past the day-to-day pressures of the organizations we've worked for.

## INTERNAL RESPONSIVENESS

Awareness of an organization's internal competencies does not guarantee a clear path to innovation. An organization may be well aware of its strengths and market demand, yet still unable to effect change within itself quickly enough to meet market requirements.

The next cell of the innovation chain, internal responsiveness, considers how quickly the collective competencies of an organization can be translated into actions that respond to a customer or market need. The key here is the ability to respond quickly and seize an opportunity in spite of the rigidity of a value chain or the lack of cooperation between the right set of partners.

## EXTERNAL RESPONSIVENESS

In any organization or industry, success is ultimately measured by the ability to respond to turbulence in a market by making decisions without having to coordinate and consider every factor in a complex business and market environment. External responsiveness is that ability to fire at once when the crosshairs of the organization's collective capabilities align with the requirements of the market. This is the essence of competitive advantage—a level of responsiveness to environmental conditions that is significantly faster than that of competitors.

## EXTERNAL AWARENESS

There's no point in responding quickly, though, if it's still too late. Like a frostbitten hiker resting a numbed hand on a hot stove, some companies may only become aware of the extent of their lack of awareness after they smell their own burning flesh. Innovative organizations, on the other hand, are wired with high levels of continuous awareness (both external and internal). External awareness represents the organization's ability to understand how the market perceives the value associated with its products and services. When coupled with internal awareness, external awareness leads to the formation of entirely new markets.

It is important to realize that external awareness involves more than extensive focus groups and market research. These can often provide false clues. They provide testimony to what the market needs today, or yesterday, rather than what it will need in the future. In the worst case it provides only the answers that the marketplace thinks you wants to hear. Even 3M's Post-it Notes, one of the most successful innovations of all time, received an initial market response from focus groups and consumers that was barely lukewarm.

## UNDERSTANDING THE INNOVATION CHAIN

To make the picture of the innovation chain clearer, here's how different organizations behave in its four stages. Figure 8 showed the innovation chain as a matrix of four cells, corresponding to the ongoing evolution of innovation. For organizations that are not innovation driven, the stages of the innovation chain look like Table 2.

### TABLE 2. THE INNOVATION CHAIN IN A NON–INNOVATION-DRIVEN ORGANIZATION

|  | Internal | External |
|---|---|---|
| **Awareness** | Ideas are stifled by a hierarchical command-and-control structure in the value chain, rigid processes, and lack of an awareness as to core competency. Ideas have no place to take root, social networking is poor, little collaboration occurs across the organization, and there is no inventory of ideas and skills. | Poor channels to manage customer relationships result in lost opportunities to mine customer experiences. No processes are in place to provide open innovation participation, and coordination among partners is poor. |
| **Responsiveness** | There are no systems to bridge geographic and cultural diversity, no internal function to connect ideas and solvers, and no form of 3M's 15 percent rule to allow for "out of task" collaboration. | Innovation cycles are far apart; extensive emphasis on internal rate of return for old products and systems stifles experimentation with new market needs. Fear of attacking current products and processes precludes market testing and fast failure. |

*Poor channels of awareness and responsiveness stifle innovation.*

TABLE 3. **THE INNOVATION CHAIN IN AN INNOVATION-DRIVEN ORGANIZATION**

|  | Internal | External |
|---|---|---|
| **Awareness** | Systems are in place to capture new ideas and inventory them, and strong social networking spreads awareness of them. The organization is collectively aware of its strengths and weaknesses and has a well-defined core competency. | The open innovation model includes an embedded ability to observe and learn from customer experience. Involvement of partners leads to rapid reconfiguration of supply chains. |
| **Responsiveness** | The organization is able to instantly organize skills and partners across current boundaries based on an unfiltered assessment of resources. People are encouraged to dedicate time to nontask work. | A fast-fail philosophy is in place. Strong relationship management systems communicate with customers, permitting a quick feedback loop to refine the approach. |

*Permeable stages create an open atmosphere for innovation.*

In organizations that are innovation driven, all four stages are permeable, allowing fast partnering and the immediate transfer of competencies, knowledge, processes, and services among and between the stages. Innovative organizations that make good use of their knowledge have characteristics in the cells that look like Table 3.

Innovation is measured by the speed and frequency with which an organization flows through these four stages. This represents an organization's velocity of innovation.

## Measuring the Velocity of Innovation

Velocity measures two very important aspects of innovation. First, how long does it take your organization to get from idea to value? Second, how frequently do you repeat the idea-to-value cycle? The result is that velocity reflects your historical ability to sustain innovation over time as opposed to the size or value of any single innovation. The higher the velocity, the better the organization has been at sustaining constant innovation in bringing new and successful products or services to market.

Since the time from idea to value and the frequency of these cycles will vary from industry to industry, no single absolute metric defines good velocity across all industries. For example, the velocity of innovation for popular fashion is very fast. We all laugh at how silly we looked in the clothes we thought so stylish in pictures taken just a few years ago. On the other hand, the velocity of innovation in the case of political systems is very slow. Many of the great democratic innovations of ancient Athens still apply in our modern-day forms of government. Our notion of democracy has changed and will continue to change, but it is still based on tenets created many centuries ago.

*Velocity measures how long it takes to get from idea to value, and how frequently that cycle repeats.*

Don't confuse the velocity of innovation with measures such as time to market (TTM). TTM measures how long it takes to bring a product from conception to commercialization. Important as this metric is, it is very subjective—it's often hard if not impossible to determine when a product or service actually came into being. Take Post-it Notes again: Was the starting point when the adhesive was discovered or when the adhesive was applied to a piece of paper? It doesn't matter. What does matter is that you don't discard ideas if they are not immediately relevant, but instead retain the ability to mine them over time. The real question is, How often can you bring new ideas to the market in a way that actually delivers measurable value? Ideas may well lie dormant for some time before that and well ahead of any actual market need. Just bringing these ideas to market faster does little to create value and may even destroy value if an idea is brought to market too fast and with poor quality, packaging, and functionality. It can be more dangerous to be first to market than to follow fast and effectively.

On the other hand, if you can demonstrate that the innovations you have brought to market (keeping in mind that these can be business model innovations just as well as products or services) are successful and generate a certain percentage of your revenues over time, you have a clear benchmark for successful innovation.

People often maintain that profit may be a better measure of success than revenue. While I agree in concept, profit is also a much harder number than revenue to arrive at for individual innovations, especially in fast-paced environments where resources are shared or spread out over a highly distributed organization. And even if you could precisely identify your own company's profit margin on a specific product, it is unlikely you would find that data readily available from other organizations for comparative purposes.

*The real question is, How often can you bring new ideas to the market in a way that actually delivers measurable value?*

Table 4 provides an example of how innovation velocity works. Take hypothetical Company 1. For the past five consecutive years it has derived 50 percent of its revenue from innovations that have been introduced in that same year. This company would have a velocity of 2.5. Not bad. However, Company 2, which has for ten years derived 100 percent of its yearly revenue from innovations introduced in the past three years, would have a velocity of 3.3. Even better.

Another way to visualize this is by picking a specific level of contribution for innovations, say, 50 percent. That would mean 50 percent of revenue over a certain period of time is generated by innovations. That makes it possible to plot the innovation velocity for an organization given different time frames for the period of "Introduction Years" (the number of years over which the innovations that contribute 50 percent of revenues have been brought to market) and the "Sustained Years" (the number of years during which you have sustained 50 percent of revenues from innovation brought to market during the past $X$ number of years). Figure 9 shows that while the Introduction Years total is important, Sustained Years is the

TABLE 4. **VELOCITY OF INNOVATION IN FOUR COMPANIES**

|  | Velocity | Profit % | Introduction Years | Sustained Years |
|---|---|---|---|---|
| **Company 1** | 2.5 | 50 | 1 | 5 |
| **Company 2** | 3.3 | 100 | 3 | 10 |
| **Company 3** | 2.3 | 70 | 3 | 10 |
| **Company 4** | 1.0 | 100 | 20 | 20 |

*The higher the velocity rating, the more innovative the company. For example, Company 2's Velocity equals Sustained Years times Profit % (converted to a numeral), divided by Introduction Years, or 3.3 = (10 x 1.0) / 3; Company 3's Velocity equals 2.3 = (10 x .7) / 3.*

FIGURE 9. **INNOVATION VELOCITY AT A 50 PERCENT CONTRIBUTION**

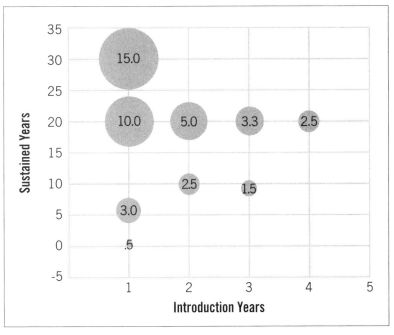

*Large bubbles indicate an organization that is able to sustain a high degree of revenue contribution for innovation over many years.*

real determinant of an organization's innovation velocity. (The size of the bubble indicates the relative velocity of innovation—the larger the bubble, the higher the velocity.)

A complete innovation velocity analysis must look at the life cycle and contribution of every product over the time period being measured, including the complexity of multiple product lines and varying revenue contributions by each line. Figure 10 shows the velocity picture of one company over four years.

However, even a simple analysis of available public data provides a clear sense for where your organization stands in its industry relative to its competitors. For example, consider that in the case of most high-technology companies at least 30 percent of revenues needs to be generated by products introduced in the prior three years, and in many cases it is reasonable to expect 80 percent of revenues to come from products introduced in the past two years. Think about the last time you walked into your favorite computer store to buy a laptop,

FIGURE 10. **VELOCITY OF INNOVATION**

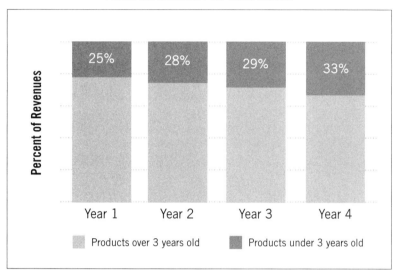

*Every organization has to sustain some baseline of innovation to compete within its industry. Between 25 percent and 33 percent of revenues for the organization in Figure 10 have resulted from products and services introduced in the past three years. Measuring this proportion is a key part of determining your payback on innovation.*

PDA, or cell phone. Would you buy anything older than twelve months? Unlikely—you'd know that you were buying outdated technology. This principle applies as much to services, business models, and internal processes as it does to products. It doesn't mean that you need to throw out every aspect of a business every two to three years. Velocity of innovation is always a relative measure. Metrics vary greatly by industry. As with any other measure of return (return on investment, internal rate of return, return on assets, and the rest) you need only do better than your competitors in your market's context to be successful.

## Enabling Innovation with Technology

When you start measuring innovation you will also undoubtedly start to think of ways in which you can further accelerate the flow of innovation, and this will lead you to ask about technology that you can use to do this. If you are this far along, congratulations—you're 90 percent of the way there! But the last 10 percent may well be the most important in today's fast-paced markets.

The last piece of an Innovation Zone tends to involve putting in place technology that will provide a way to handle the life cycle of ideas and also to enable them in the fastest possible way once you're ready to put them into practice.

While technology can help accelerate innovation in many ways, there are two areas where it can have the most significant impact: innovation management systems and agile process innovation.

## INNOVATION MANAGEMENT SYSTEMS

Innovation software tools offer a platform to collect, evaluate, inventory, and track ideas across an organization and its partners or customers. The simplest way to describe these tools is to compare them to an employee suggestion box. The significant difference between a physical or digital inbox and an innovation management system is that ideas submitted via an inbox (of any sort) are rarely mined over time. If an idea is timely it may be put into practice. But it's unlikely that an idea that does not address a current problem or is less than fully formed will stand much chance of being used later. An idea like the adhesive eventually used for Post-it Notes, an idea in search of a solution, is exactly the sort of idea that would be discarded in most cases without a means to inventory it for mining in the future.

*The significant difference between a physical or digital inbox and an innovation management system is that ideas submitted via an inbox are rarely mined over time.*

The approach many organizations are starting to take to deal with the flow of ideas is generally termed "innovation management." While this can be done using technology solutions already in place, such as databases and intranets, managing innovation often requires more structure, tracking, and workflow control than is available in most existing information systems.

In addition, increased volume has a dramatic impact on the processes that underpin the most basic aspects of an industry. The same is true of innovation. Many of the systems that underpin the modern organization were not designed to take advantage of volumes of data anything like what the current world throws at them. Any look at the means by which innovation can be managed in today's organizations must consider the sheer numbers, magnitude, and complexity of current problems.

It is hard to imagine that sophisticated functions now handled by electronic communications were once performed with paper. Yet, until the mid-1960s, almost all air traffic control in the United States was managed manually. Paper slips containing an airliner's flight number, navigational bearing, and destination were handed from controller to controller. In the period from 1945 to 1955, the number of domestic airline passengers rose from 6.7 million to 38 million per year. Yet only two radar-controlled air route systems were in place! The point is simply that as scale and volume of transactions in any industry increases, the volume of potential innovations will also increase. In this case the absence of an innovation management system creates a high likelihood that innovations will not find their way into practice in an organization that has been innovative at a smaller scale.

Johnson Controls, for example, is a 120-year-old company with a long legacy of innovation in environmental controls, automotive systems, and manufacturing. From the first patent for an electric thermostat to the first computer-controlled smart building, Johnson Controls has accumulated a vast warehouse of intellectual property, patents, and ideas.[1]

*If an idea requires new information systems or modifications to older ones, that idea is only as good and as timely as our ability to build the technology to support it.*

However, the company realized that its intellectual assets were not being well utilized because of the tremendous geographic dispersion of its offices and people. Intellectual assets were handled differently by each of its global businesses, severely limiting the ability to combine and collaborate on ideas. As with Sony and the MP3 market, such internal differences can have dramatic repercussions for an organization's ability to respond to the market with the full power of its innovative capacity.

To provide a common platform for innovation Johnson Controls turned to a package called Innovator, which provided a means to not only manage the existing patent portfolio but also track new ideas through their life cycle as they matured and developed. Ultimately this created an innovation discipline for Johnson Controls and significantly enhanced its ability to manage innovation as well as lower its overall cost of innovation.

According to Johnson Controls' Beth Anderson, a regional portfolio manager, "We can now act more like a global company. Innovators can view their ideas; a new feedback loop now exists. We can see everything that is going on, including how and why decisions are made. For the first time we can analyze our decision making."

The other side of enabling technology through innovation is to create an organization that can itself adapt quickly to a new business idea. The greatest idea is not worth much if the organization cannot change its practices and processes quickly enough to integrate it into its business. While some of this is clearly cultural, much of it is also technical. If an idea requires new information systems or modifications to older ones, that idea is only as good and as timely as our ability to build the technology to support it.

This last point gets into a much more involved discussion about the basic agility of an organization's information and technology systems. For instance, are these systems agile enough to allow for quick reengineering? Does the organization's technology allow users to make changes to processes on their own? Can customers quickly and easily customize processes to suit their needs? This can open up a hornet's nest of challenges. But I have seen ways in which organizations are addressing these issues, with a specific eye toward how quickly they can innovate internal systems to handle external demands for innovation.

## AGILE PROCESS INNOVATION

It's very difficult not to introduce technology into the innovation discussion. For the typical business a change in any process requires a change in the technology that supports the process. Technology also divides organizations into two opposing camps: those believing that technology slows innovation because of the many standards and rules that need to be followed to implement technology change, and those believing that it accelerates innovation since it formalizes a process change and ensures that it is adhered to. But that dichotomy was born in a time when technology had to be rigid and well defined if it were to be deployed with any degree of quality and reliability. In today's world, technology and innovation are no longer part of a zero-sum game; you can have bulletproof rules and standards while allowing for free-form innovation. Marrying these two objectives calls for reconstituting business components to suit an organization's needs at any given time.

It used to be that for a business to respond to any new market condition it had to define a new set of requirements to its information

technology staff, who would then attempt to reduce these requirements to technology specifications that could be used to write code
in a programming language and so provide a solution. However, this
process simply takes too long for the pace of modern business, especially a service business that relies on its ability to quickly innovate
new ways to serve customers in an effort to differentiate what is otherwise a commodity service. One alternative to this tedious and
drawn-out approach is to define the pieces of each business process as
single technology objects that can then be combined with other
objects to create a new application much faster. The analogy would be
building a new assembly line for each new feature of an automobile
as opposed to simply reconfiguring the assembly line by using robots
that can use a number of different routines to assemble any configu-
ration of car. In the case of a business process it's a bit more complex,
since the new configurations aren't known until they come along,
whereas the options for an automobile are already known. However,
if you can establish a library of these recombinable parts or business
objects, you can then innovate new configurations with increasing
ease.

Each business object in this framework has reliability and predictability within its small and finite purview. But the objects—which
are nothing more than small collections of process rules—
can combine in infinite ways to create responses to new
and unforeseen opportunities and challenges. The repository of objects, built over time, can become a significant
innovation enabler, especially in larger organizations
where existing process steps end up buried in years of
legacy systems and procedures and, because they are
tightly integrated with large technology applications, cannot be
extracted and used as separate recombinable objects.

*Technology and
innovation are no
longer part of a
zero-sum game.*

The result of a rules-based innovation capability is a powerful
lever for dealing with unanticipated opportunities in novel ways. This
capability becomes the foundation of a solid innovation competency
since it allows an organization to act on an opportunity by quickly
creating new business processes. While many other organizations
may see the opportunity at the same time, almost all of them will use
existing processes for their responses, which simply force-fits a less-
than-optimal solution. If instead you are able to provide novel and
innovative solutions to a new and unanticipated market need, you
can significantly outpace your competition.

## Innovation Recap

It is possible and desirable to measure the value of innovation and technology's role in the Innovation Zone. A key index of this is velocity of innovation.

Velocity measures two very important aspects of innovation. First, how long does it take your organization to get from idea to value? Second, how frequently do you repeat the idea-to-value cycle? The velocity of innovation is measured and improved by using a model called the *innovation chain*. Four stages determine the velocity of an innovation chain:

- Internal awareness

- Internal responsiveness

- External responsiveness

- External awareness

The faster an organization can traverse the four stages of the innovation chain, the better its ability to innovate.

Two key technologies can help you accelerate and manage innovation: innovation management systems and agile process innovation. An innovation management system provides a technology that can be used to capture idea submissions, help in evaluating ideas, and facilitate the entire life cycle of activities involved in managing innovations. Agile process innovation provides a technology that allows an organization to define the many aspects of its business processes as a set of rules that can be combined with infinite variability, making it possible to respond to the market quickly with new business processes, products, and services.

CHAPTER **8**

# GLOBALIZATION AND A NATIONAL INNOVATION AGENDA

*Several years ago I was in my Boston office speaking with a researcher who was helping me with a previous book. He was a graduate student from India who was studying at a local university. As we talked about globalization, the topic turned to U.S. economics. I described the growing concern about the U.S. economy and the prospects for its position as a leader in the future. I asked him what concerns he and his Indian colleagues had, expecting an answer about the cultural and social chasms that were being formed in India as the result of the recent surge in prosperity from outsourcing. Instead he looked out from the twenty-seventh floor overlooking the Boston skyline and said, as he pointed to the hundreds of office buildings that lined the streets below, "This is what concerns me. What will happen to the U.S. economy. Because if you falter, we all suffer."*

Those comments have haunted me on many occasions since that meeting. It is simpleminded to think of an economic downturn anywhere in a developed economy around the globe not having severe repercussions across the globe.

The global economy is not about cutting costs, eliminating jobs, and sending work offshore. These are the early nervous tics and restless twitches five minutes into a twenty-four-hour game of poker. If

151

we play to these short-sighted drivers today, we will not only exhaust ourselves before the first few hands but (worse yet) we will destroy our ability to compete in the long-term reshaping of the global economy and the prosperity of our children's role in it.

I remember being invited to present to the CEO and the top sixty execs of one of America's leading banks. The topic, of course, was innovation. I was concerned; it was not the best time to be talking about innovation in banking. The U.S. financial markets were reeling from the impact of the subprime lending crisis, and central banks around the world were starting to funnel money, lots of money (close to $500 billion at that early point), into their member banks to avoid a credit meltdown. The CEO told me that in thirty years of banking he had yet to see a crisis with the potential to cause as much disruption and damage in the industry.

Despite the market distraction, it's in times of crisis that most reformation and innovation occurs. What struck me most in my discussions with these senior banking execs was the global nature of the current crisis. It used to be that if one country's or region's financial system cycled down another would cycle up. Big money has been playing the global arbitrage game for years. Global markets weren't completely isolated from each other, but they were separated by just enough reasonable distance, geographically and economically, to allow inefficiencies to arise. In free markets inefficiencies create opportunities for inequity, which, bluntly put, means someone prospers at someone else's expense. But the efficiency of globally connected financial markets has created a fear that we are living in a global economy that is offering less and less refuge to weather a storm. My feeling is different. What we are building is a new level of economic interreliance, which will provide a hedge against uncertainty and volatility. However, this new level of interreliance and economic dependence between nations comes with a steep price: It demands a relentless capacity to innovate.

*Despite the market distraction, it's in times of crisis that most reformation and innovation occurs.*

This is a trend that has been at least fifty years in the making, dating back to the idea of the global village popularized by Marshall McLuhan, but it is not until recently that we have started to realize the true potential of moving work electronically across the globe to whatever location and whatever talent is best suited for it. This trend to move work wherever it can be most economically accomplished is undoubtedly the single greatest innovation of the twenty-first century.

## Global Innovation

However, globalization is still not being used to directly drive innovation. At best it serves to offload noncore activities so that an organization can focus on its core. Helpful as that is, it does not change the innovation process in any substantial way.

One of the biggest breakthroughs that will take shape in the next era of global sourcing has to do with the fundamental motivators to do it in the first place. Today most U.S. companies still see globalization strictly as a way to derive massive savings from the dramatic reduction in labor costs in India, Russia, Eastern Europe, and the Pacific Rim, and the reduced cycle times possible when another workforce is active while the domestic workforce sleeps.

That hasn't changed much throughout the growth of the globalization phenomenon. Delphi research results show that today cost is still the single greatest factor in making a sourcing decision. However, while these immediate savings continue to play a vital role in the attraction to global sourcing, it is becoming clear that direct cost benefits are fleeting at best and an outright illusion at worst. Global teams create levels of complexity in management, metrics, and productivity whose cost sometimes offsets the predicted savings and often stifles innovation across a company and an industry trapped in the silos created by sourcing relationships.

The challenge in both cases, offshore and onshore, lies in the growing complexity of sourcing. We have, in many ways, exceeded the capacity of the frameworks we use to manage sourcing at its current scale. But that's not all. Delphi research also shows that two other factors, in addition to cost, are fast approaching top-tier status as driving forces in a sourcing decision: faster time to market and access to global innovation networks. This is where the greatest shift in attitudes and drivers of sourcing will occur in the next decade.

So sharpen your pencil—here is some simple math I want you to check. In the U.S. labor market:

*Globalization at best serves to offload noncore activities. Helpful as that is, it does not change the innovation process in any substantial way.*

- College-educated boomers to retire by 2020: 46 million

- College-educated workers to enter the workforce by 2020: 49 million

- New skilled positions to be introduced by 2020: 12 million

All told, these numbers purport to show, we will have a net deficit of nine million workers in the U.S. economy by the year 2020.[1]

Does it add up for you? Not for me.

I hear a great deal about the coming skill shortage in the United States. Jobs are being sent offshore, and the kids are shying away from math, science, engineering, IT, and technical professions partly because they see the jobs leaving and partly because teachers for these professions are growing scarce as baby boomers retire from teaching.

*The perception is that demand for technical skills will dry up in the same way that the demand for manufacturing skills has. As a result, technical skills are being actively discouraged as a career option.*

All of this is well founded and the math works. Unfortunately, as with most attempts to predict the future by reducing it to numbers representative of past experiences, it leaves out new variables that find their way into the equation and radically alter it.

So what is the variable in this case? Before I offer a suggestion, I need to spell out the magnitude of the crisis based on what we now know.

## A NONVIRTUOUS CYCLE

The United States is indeed hemorrhaging technical skills to the rest of the world, although in a world with increasingly permeable borders that shouldn't surprise anyone. What may surprise you is that our schools are falling far behind in terms of sheer numbers when it comes to the students who are choosing a technical career. At first this shows up as a shift to cheaper offshore workers. This in turn creates the onshore illusion that we actually need fewer technical graduates. So we respond to the deficit in technical staff by going offshore even more aggressively. The unintended consequence is that this only increases the pay scale of offshored work and further reduces the need for onshore talent. That's a repeating cycle not to be easily dismissed. It feeds on itself because the more we send offshore the less attractive these disciplines become as career options and the higher we drive the cost of offshore labor, and all the while the onshore skills gap increases.

The perception of youth, parents, and education counselors is that demand for technical skills will dry up in the same way that the demand for manufacturing skills has. As a result, technical skills are being actively discouraged as a career option.

The liability this creates is huge. As wages for these skills climb, as they are already doing outside the United States, wage arbitrage is

mitigated or potentially eliminated and onshore companies begin to look for onshore talent to supplement
higher-end skill sets. This is already happening in manufacturing, where U.S. companies simply can't find the talent they need onshore. It will undoubtedly happen in
many other areas as well. It already is. If you don't believe
me, then talk to the large high-tech players who are doing
their damnedest to get high school kids excited about a
tech career. Microsoft, for instance, is doing road shows
across the country touting high-tech careers and giving
away Xboxes in order to get these kids excited about a
technology career.

*With the benefit of being able to move work anywhere on the globe and the increasing sophistication and capacity of global higher education, the real boom time for global innovation is just getting ready to begin*

It it were just a matter of offshoring commodity skills,
the issue wouldn't be worthy of much concern. However,
globalization is rapidly maturing to take higher ground in areas of research and development. With the benefit of being able to move work
anywhere on the globe and the increasing sophistication and capacity of global higher education, the real boom time for global innovation is just getting ready to begin. We just happen to be at the cusp of
this transformation as globalization takes hold. When the real boom
gets here we will be woefully unprepared to take advantage of the opportunity if we keep to the current trajectory.

Look at it this way: For every job being sent offshore at least 1.5
new jobs are being created in higher-level skills for technical architecture, coordination, and innovation. And that ratio is growing, from
what I can project. This creates a new set of opportunities for those
with a ready pool of technical talent.

So here's the question that should keep us up at night. Who will
own the skills gap? Who will step up to the plate and be the world's
innovator?

Here's some food for thought to help you understand the magnitude of the predicament and to form your own answers. The U.S.
Census Bureau's 2008 database provides information to graph population pyramids for many regions of the world, highlighting the way
demographics are going to shape the workforce of the future. Figures
11 and 12 show the picture for the United States in 2000 and 2025.

The 2000 U.S. pyramid shows a bulge in the working age population bands. This pear-shaped demographic pattern is typical for most
industrialized nations. In theory the bulge should move through the
pyramid—think of the image of a snake swallowing its prey whole.

FIGURE 11. **POPULATION PYRAMID: UNITED STATES (2000)**

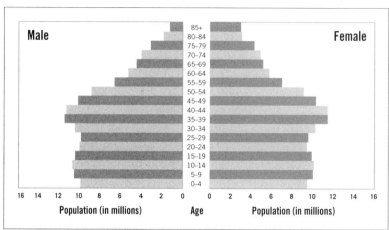

FIGURE 12. **POPULATION PYRAMID: UNITED STATES (2025)**

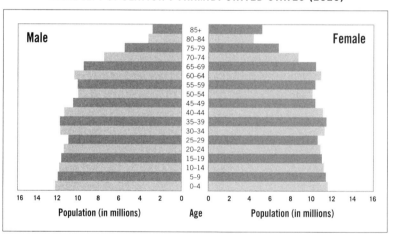

However, the current reality is that as the bulge moves up, the lower age bands fill out as well; see the U.S. pyramid for 2025. In addition, the working age population does not increase in terms of total number of workers. This creates a host of social issues, including a larger population to educate at the base of the pyramid and a larger population to care for at the top. If the same number of workers are supporting a larger overall population with a higher percentage of social welfare needs, the economic impact will be substantial. And to fund

FIGURE 13. **POPULATION PYRAMID: INDIA (2000)**

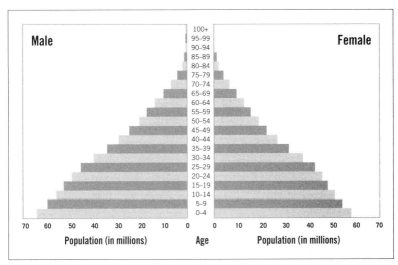

FIGURE 14. **POPULATION PYRAMID: INDIA (2025)**

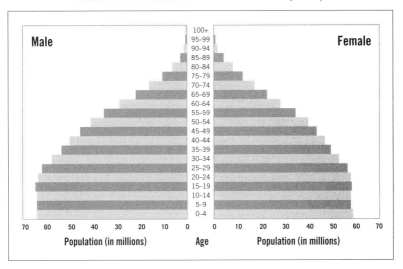

that impact, our only options are to increase national debt and to increase national productivity. Clearly the latter is preferred if we want to maintain the strength of the U.S. economy. But this can't be done without a national commitment to innovation.

Next consider the pyramids for India, in Figures 13 and 14.

India's present age demographics reflect the classic pyramid shape, which is more typical of a developing economy, where birth rates are high but life span is relatively short on average across the population. However, when you roll the clock forward to 2025 the change is dramatic. The Indian workforce will start to fill in the growing resource needs of a globalized economy, creating a feeder for its workforce that may dominate the century. Granted, it's not that easy. Infrastructure, education, and health care all present enormous challenges for India. But an expanding workforce may bring capital into India that, if applied intelligently, could quickly start to turn these challenges around.

But wait, what about China? While we have heard a great deal about the size of the Chinese population, the demographics for 2025 tell a different long-term story. A clear bulge is going through China's working age population, as seen in Figure 15, but China's pyramid is also shrinking at the bottom. This may not have an impact in the next twenty years as these youngsters move into the workforce, but it most certainly will impact China's competitive position in competing for global work beyond that. Again the same issues of infrastructure and education that plague India also face China.

FIGURE 15. **POPULATION PYRAMID: CHINA (2025)**

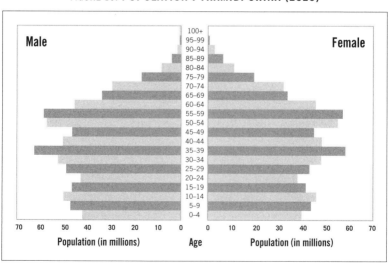

## WHAT DOES IT ALL MEAN?

What does all this mean? In short, for the next two decades, the United States will desperately need to increase productivity and augment its workforce to allow its economy to grow and meet the social needs of many more younger and older citizens. At the same time, India and China will battle it out for global position. Beyond that, India will have a huge share of the global workforce. By the way, although the phenomenon is most pronounced in India, especially given its population size, Latin American countries such as Brazil and Mexico are also growing into economic powerhouses with population pyramids that reflect India's profile of a continuously expanding base.

However all this plays out, we will most certainly be in for some serious reengineering of our education and social welfare systems—as though you didn't have enough to think about.

America is already reeling from the complacency demonstrated when the automotive industry was reinvented by Japanese manufacturing. While I acknowledge that Ford and GM today are finally proclaiming the benefits of innovation and espousing the virtues of the U.S. worker, they should also be held firmly accountable for coming to the party twenty years late. Manufacturing productivity has increased in every industrial nation, with output and employment keeping step, whether you look at Japan, Germany, Brazil, or the United States. We will not stem this tide of the past two decades. Innovation may be our national core competency, but it is extraordinarily difficult for the U.S. automobile industry to prove it.

If we want to avoid a similar wholesale sellout of the services industry as well, then we need to start investing in innovation as a core competency for the next two decades of global competition now, not in 2026.

The way to do this is amazingly straightforward and involves a commitment to a national agenda that focuses on renewing our preeminence in education, developing new mechanisms for protecting intellectual property, and emphasizing eco-friendly innovation.

*Education is ultimately the foundation of an innovation economy.*

# The Innovation Agenda

The first time I met Peter Drucker was over lunch in his hometown of Claremont. We spent several hours talking about a multitude of topics.

When the conversation turned to technology I asked him if he thought the accelerating speed of innovation was due to advances in information technology. Drucker's response, as was typical, delved into the history of the answer, but it also opened a door to what I believe is one of the most essential insights on the increasing drive toward higher levels of innovation in every industry, education:

> I think you underrate the change in the workforce. The change in the workforce came first with the GI Bill of Rights. Harry Truman was ready to go to college when his father went bankrupt in 1911—Harry had to take over the farm. All of his life he was disappointed he could not go to college. Yet when the Bill of Rights came up, the august president of Harvard University (his education adviser) came back and said, "You don't have to worry— no one will take advantage of the GI Bill." Sixty percent [of those eligible] did. And this came before the technological revolution.

The role of education is clear in fostering not only the attitudes and behaviors for innovation but also the methods and mechanisms needed to make it a process. Education is ultimately the foundation of an innovation economy. And it is a process that starts in kindergarten and continues through all stages of education. However, far too often education serves to teach us that there is only one solution, one answer to each question. In a simpler time with less complex problems, that approach served us well. But as the world's problems have multiplied and intertwined and as we face more ambitious challenges in health care, the environment, energy, and so many other areas, education is not keeping pace. We should not fear innovation in education any more than we should fear innovation in business. The good news is that the change has started—in pockets, in nooks and crannies, but it is a start nonetheless.

*Innovation can be taught. This has always been the core competency of America.*

First, we must embark on a long-term process of reinvention in how we educate and prepare our children for competition in a global innovation economy. This is basic table stakes. Yet many of today's classrooms and schools are designed to drive innovation out of children. With standardized testing at the forefront of public education, class sizes burgeoning, and teachers unable to deliver one-to-one attention to students, we are failing to set a benchmark for world-class education. Innovation can be taught and bright-eyed creativity can be fostered in the next generation of thought leaders on the global stage. In many ways this has always been the core competency of America. Our universities are still the envy of the world, attracting students from every other nation. Our ability to insource research, development, and engineering still creates more jobs than outsourcing takes away. Yet we are losing the edge. India is already graduating more engineering students than the United States. Japan has a higher percentage of its eligible population attending university than we do. If we are to keep our edge, we need to take these threats seriously.

*It's nice when your kids think enough of you to share their view of the world, but I walk away from these encounters feeling as though I am forever falling behind.*

At times it feels as though we're looking into a rearview mirror watching the world catch up even though we're going at top speed. What's encouraging, however, is that kids today are already adopting a new view of innovation by sheer virtue of the context they have been immersed in. I see it constantly in the behavior of my own children and those I interact with.

Some time ago I came across a YouTube video about kinetic sculptor Theo Jansen. His work is the ideal mash-up of innovation, creativity, engineering, and art. His sculptures are made of conventional materials such as wood, plastic bottles, and string and are powered by the wind. But these are not kites or simple machines, they are massive in scale—dwarfing a human being—and walk elegantly on multiple legs like graceful gigantic spiders. One of the first things I did after viewing the video was to call my eleven-year-old daughter over to watch it. She was duly impressed. But, as is usually the case whenever I try to impress her with my techno-savvy, she immediately turned around and decided to show me the dozens of similar YouTube videos she had already uncovered. It's nice when your kids think enough of you to actually share their view of the world, but I inevitably walk away from these encounters feeling as though I am forever falling behind. It seems that my leading edge is held back by some kind of generational hobble, while her leading edge knows no such restraint.

The only consolation here is that I am far from alone. My experience has consistently reinforced my perception of a growing rift between generations around the topic of innovation. Kids see innovation as being something that happens in a million small increments each day. They are not daunted by innovation because for them innovation is not a boil-the-ocean strategy. Those of us on the other side of the generational divide look for big-bang innovations. We grew up in a world where inventions took decades to develop and decades to grow. These kids have experienced a world where innovation is rampant, happening in increments of weeks, days, even hours.

Kids today are also living in an open model of the world—a model that is not confined by closed systems of innovation. Their laboratory has no walls, no organization. They interact with each other across every boundary we have regarded as sacrosanct, whether it's an office door, an enterprise organization chart, or a national border. Watch the way open systems from software development such as Linux and Wikipedia have taken hold and you catch a glimpse of this. This new generation accepts that innovation involves thousands of pieces of ideas, in millions of pieces of gray matter, that can somehow form spontaneously into new stuff—cool stuff and useful stuff. We (those of us slightly older) don't want to believe that. We want to engineer change. We want to architect innovation. We want to control invention. If you feel your defenses rising and your blood boiling as you read this, then you and I know exactly which side of the generational chasm you're on. If not, then stay young!

This is especially evident watching the way marketing is evolving as a leading indicator of social attitudes toward innovation and change. This dramatic shift just about turns classic marketing on its head. Much of today's Web-based marketing is crude, inexpensive, personal, instantaneous, and horribly temporal. It's what's come to be called *managed spontaneity,* and virtually every company trying to reach the under-twenty demographic is turning to it through social networking.

*Kids today interact with each other across every boundary that we have regarded as sacrosanct.*

"But that's just marketing," you may well think. "Real innovation of products is different; it takes much more structure." Don't get stuck in products. Remember, innovation *is* the process.

I'm not saying that innovation and change do not need architecture, forethought, or effort. They do, but not as we once knew it. In software development the "agile" movement is a good analogy. It used to be that you would build software and then, once you knew what the software was supposed to do, you would build a test case to see if it worked. Today the technology of software development is so open and rapid that the tests have to be written before the software is written. Ready—fire—aim, as the saying goes.

As much as I talk about innovation, I have to wonder how much of what it's ultimately evolving into I will never really understand, can never really understand, because I've just been wired in a different way by my education and experience.

But the bottom line is inescapable. You just can't innovate in this new world using old ideas of innovation any better than you can mess with quantum engineering using Newtonian physics. If we want to stay and play in the Innovation Zone, we had better educate our children to manage spontaneity and thrive on it.

So where is that being done? In more places than you might think and many more than I could list here. Following are just two of the leading lights in the area of innovation, programs that I have already seen make a difference in creating a model for the education of future generations.

## DESTINATION IMAGINATION

One of the avenues for many school-age children to gain exposure and experience in the skills of innovation is outside the classroom. Knoxville, Tennessee, is not the first place that comes to mind when you hear the word *innovation,* but for a few days each year it is a center for thousands of eager young minds who gather to redefine innovation for the rest of us.

Knoxville is the home of the global competition for Destination ImagiNation. Destination ImagiNation (DI) is a creative problem-solving program targeted to K–12 that has trained more than seven million children worldwide on the techniques, methods, discipline, and process of creative problem solving. Five million of these children are employed in the United States today—representing approximately 3 percent of our workforce!

The program was started twenty-five years ago by a prior organization with a similar mission, Odyssey of the Mind. The intent behind the program is to teach children how to think and act creatively when faced with challenges. These take the form of what are called *instant* and *central challenges.*

My own involvement with this program began six years ago when my daughter, Mia, was entering kindergarten. Mia showed a definite propensity for math, engineering, and science, and I was damned if I

*Nothing is more contagious than the unbounded enthusiasm of kids presented with a challenge.*

was going to let that enthusiasm get squashed by the stereotyping of kids by grade school educators who thought little girls didn't fit that mold.

I found out about DI and immediately went to an orientation with Mia. What impressed me was the way the program stressed a process of creativity, teamwork, and tools that went far beyond what kids are taught in the classroom or on the playing field.

Nothing is more contagious than the unbounded enthusiasm of kids presented with a challenge. They are undaunted by obstacles, see only opportunity, and still find more reason why something should work than why it shouldn't.

DI presents kids with challenges in a variety of forms. Some of these challenges last an entire season and culminate in an end-of-season tournament. These are their "central challenges": complex exercises in innovation that have infinite solutions. Others are called "instant challenges" and last only a few minutes. These challenges are meant to reflect the spontaneity of dealing with uncertainty in an innovative and highly collaborative fashion.

A central challenge might involve building a structure to hold weight. In one case the challenge was to build a structure seven to nine inches tall using no more than fourteen grams of wood (that's the weight of about two pencils), to design it in such a way that it consisted of two structures, one inside the other, and to make sure the two structures weighed within two grams of the same amount. The structure would then be tested to see how much weight it could hold. Take two pencils and think to yourself how much weight your structure could hold. The structures I saw in the global competition held anywhere from three hundred to a thousand pounds. Yikes! To put that into perspective, the ratio of fourteen grams to a thousand pounds would scale up to a ten-pound wooden structure holding in excess of *324,000* pounds of weight.

Impressive? Sure it is. But not half as impressive as seeing the undaunted confidence in the eyes of these kids and the way they approach innovation as a process that requires tools and methods. For them the word *innovation* does not carry the stigma of rarity and serendipity that it does for most of us. They see innovation as a constant process of discovery. They live innovation in the way they collaborate. When I asked one team how it was that they came up with good ideas, their answer floored me: "We try to get different kids on our team. The more diverse we are, the better our solution." Now there's something we should all know intuitively. But for most adults today the first thing that comes to mind when they hear "diversity" is conflict.

*Teams used to be things you went to twice a week to be part of. For these kids teams are what you are 24/7.*

Sorry to break it to you, but our image of teams is outdated. Your superhero was an army of one. Their superheroes are teams.

Team play to those of us over the age of twenty was never really taught off the playing field. Sure, we learned how to play off a rulebook for sports. But how many of us were taught how to play without a rulebook in life? The process of team play for these kids is second nature. They live in an IM-linked, always-on team where agility and responsiveness are built into the fabric of their lives. Teams used to be things you went to twice a week to be part of. For these kids teams are what you are 24/7.

But educating the next generation on innovation does not end at grade 12. Our universities and postsecondary schools need to also change the approach they take to teaching innovation as an integrated discipline. That too is starting to take shape.

## THE EDUCATION IS FREE; THE REWARDS ARE PRICELESS

What might that sort of a school look like? Imagine a world-class engineering college that provides each and every student with a full four-year scholarship to the tune of $150,000. This school also has shunned classrooms for the unconventional setup of labs in every class that provide hands-on use of the latest technology from day one. First-year students get to use electron scanning microscopes, mass spectrometers, injection molding machines, laser welders, and many more devices that most engineering students only get to see in textbook pictures—if that. This setup is combined with experiential learning and project-based work three to four times that of other engineering schools.

*The mission: Create a new breed of engineers who understand the process of innovation and can adapt quickly to the uncertainty of new technologies and new challenges.*

Students at this school also work with major multinationals to create innovative products, services, and processes that the R&D labs of these multibillion-dollar companies have not been able to develop on their own, all as part of their schooling. Companies actually line up to fund these projects. Many of these collaborative innovations create multimillion-dollar enhancements or products for their sponsors. But wait, there's more! This school is also partnered with one of the world's leading business colleges in order to provide truly integrated innovation skills and education on entrepreneurism and business.

All this sounds like some sort of idealized view of the future of higher education in innovation—but it's not. This school exists today, and it's not located in India or China. It's not one of the standard candidates such as MIT or Stanford. It's Olin College, located in the sleepy town of Needham, Massachusetts, and its story is one of the best-kept secrets in higher education—but also one of the most insightful views of what the future of innovation may look like.

Olin's mission is to create a new breed of engineers who understand the process of innovation and have the ability to quickly adapt to the uncertainty of new technologies and new challenges. That sounds like any other engineering school until you walk into its classrooms and see the tremendous emphasis placed on experience at Olin.

Yet even with a renewed emphasis on education, two more significant challenges remain for us to address.

## Protecting Innovation

We need to update the patent system. We need protection for intellectual property rights that offers much more incentive to share ideas in an open market and greater assurance that these ideas will deliver value to their creators.

One of the economic precepts of modern society, free markets, and capitalism is the inalienable right of the individual to the ownership of property. We take that so much for granted in the developed world that we rarely think of what life would be like without it. However, travel to parts of the world where property ownership is a distant dream and you realize how important this is as a cornerstone of economic stability and prosperity. The Peruvian economist Hernando DeSoto has written extensively on this topic, claiming that it is one of the most fundamental requirements for economic growth.[2]

I would extend DeSoto's premise to the innovation economy as well. If we expect to build on the idea of open and collaborative innovation, we need to put in place international mechanisms to protect a new sort of intellectual property, which exists at a much more granular level than traditional patents. This is a daunting task, but no more so than patent law was at the turn of the twentieth century when the great explosion of technology inventions occurred.

In some ways this may be easier than earlier attempts to protect intellectual property rights. The World Wide Web acts as an enormous repository for history in a way we never could have imagined a hundred years ago. Organizations such as the nonprofit Internet Archive (www.archive.org) are already creating vast warehouses of Web content that act as a historical time machine allowing you to navigate back in time to see the Web as it was. While it doesn't have an exhaustive record of every single Web page that ever was, it does offer a glimpse into the sorts of resources that will be available to trace ownership of ideas.

*The World Wide Web acts as an enormous repository for history in a way we never could have imagined a hundred years ago.*

This also provides a higher bar for individuals who are tempted to abscond with ideas. The simple transparency of the Internet may self-govern much of this. In fact, it's possible to make a claim that the changing number of Nobel prizes awarded to teams is partially a function of the effect online transparency is already having in forcing collaboration rather than homesteading on the intellectual property of others.

However, don't discount the way in which the economic formula for intellectual property might change. Young people today clearly believe that sharing and open collaboration on new ideas have an inherent value that far outweighs the risk of losing rights to their individual ideas. That may sound like idealistic but immature thinking that will change as they get older and realize the value of their intellectual property, but don't be too quick to dismiss it.

Collaboration does have merit, especially in a context of uncertainty. The question becomes, Where is the best place to draw the line between the value of an individual's idea as opposed to the value of a collaborative idea? Answering that question and putting in place the mechanisms, social and legislative, to handle the implications will be something that is sure to occupy us for some time.

## Green Innovation

Think seriously about the impact of innovation on the environment. Far too many ideas end up being created in the absence of any assessment of what they will do to the living world. While enormous strides have been made in recycling, abuse of the ecology in the name of innovation is still widespread. The technology industry is especially to blame with its rapid-fire creation of less expensive and more tantalizing computers, PDAs, cell phones, and other gadgetry. The solutions here will require as much innovation as any other aspect of the tech industry.

*We may compete in a global economy, but the vast majority of people live, spend, and prosper in a local economy.*

One of the most obvious solutions is to depart from the current consumer model for electronic devices, which requires you to purchase a new cell phone, PDA, or PC every year or two. We have reached a breaking point where the sheer economics of owning electronics, from computers and TV displays to cell phones and PDAs, no longer makes sense. The value is not the platform, in terms of the materials, but rather the service it delivers. The physical device has simply become packaging for the service. We are long overdue for a technology vendor to sell the service and take responsibility for the disposal and recycling of the components. I for one would be glad to buy a yearly service from Apple that guaranteed delivery of the latest laptop, even if that involved a premium. We already lease cars. The vast majority of cell phones are free with any service contract. We simply need to price the disposal of products into the cost of innovation. We already do that, but now the price is paid in other ways as we pass on the burden of the ecological impact to future generations.

Is this national innovation agenda starting to sound *too* nationalistic? It shouldn't. Many aspects of an economy remain fundamentally national, no matter how globalized our businesses. Taxes, public and social services, health care, public education, and environmental impact and cleanup are all national issues. We may compete in a global economy, but the vast majority of people live, spend, and prosper from day to day in a local economy. If we are to do both well, then we need to balance national interests with global economics.

It's also narrow-minded to view a national policy for innovation as zero-sum with global progress in how all nations innovate. None of what I'm proposing speaks to insulation of the United States or any other nation. Without a national agenda for every nation that significantly invests in education, workforce retooling, and immigration policy, and that acknowledges the importance of building a new generation of work founded on innovation, we are heading for many decades of economic pain. With an agenda in place we significantly up the ante and create long-term prosperity for our children on a truly global scale.

## Innovation Recap

Globalization has a deep impact on the future state of innovation. We need to put in place a national agenda to help position the United States for its place in the global innovation economy.

The first point to understand is that we are living in a global economy in which there is less and less refuge to weather a storm and greater economic interreliance between nations.

Second, although globalization is still not driving innovation directly, it is inevitable that higher education in developing nations and the coming skill shortage in the United States will increase the emphasis on offshore labor. To counter this, the United States needs to dedicate itself to a renewed commitment to innovation in education, both K–12 and university.

Third, we need to put in place new mechanisms for protecting innovation as well as new attitudes to help us in sharing the raw material of ideas needed to accelerate innovation.

Finally, we need to commit ourselves to innovation that recognizes its impact on the environment. Green innovation has to become part of the discipline and expectation of innovation if we are to avoid irreversible damage from rampant inventiveness, which has characterized the better part of the twentieth century.

# EPILOGUE

*Around here, however, we don't look back for very long. We keep moving forward, opening up new doors and doing new things, because we're curious . . . and curiosity keeps leading us down new paths.* —WALT DISNEY*

So we've arrived. Are you ready to build your Innovation Zone? Do you know what it will take to get ready? If it hasn't become apparent yet, allow me to simplify. We can analyze how we got to this age of uncertainty and complexity, we can dissect the underlying causes for another few hundred pages, or we can get to work and start putting in place the ideas and methods that will enable us to create and sustain a culture of innovation in our organizations and in our lives.

It's tough work. It involves disruption and change, neither of which is a welcome participant in most lives. However, it's not as though we have a choice in the matter. But, for the sake of argument, let's say you did—what would your choice be?

It's tempting to want to roll the clock back, isn't it? You can if you've passed that precarious point where the rewards of protecting the past outweigh the risks of building the future. Some days, I'm there as well. But then I talk to people building the future, like Chet Huber at OnStar, Alph Bingham at InnoCentive, and Colin Angle at iRobot—bright-eyed, undaunted innovators who are fearless in their pursuit of tomorrow—and I realize how much an idea can change the world, not just because it is different but because it does create value and meaning.

That's when it dawns on me that so much has been invented yet so little has changed. In the past two hundred years we have laid a foundation for innovation in business, economy, technology, and culture. At times it seems to be a fragile foundation as we try to adapt it to the uncertainty of the fast-changing world around us, but it is a foundation. We have the ability to form global communities instantly; our machines can create an endless variety of products, and our organizations can take whatever form we wish. What remains is to pull all this into the twenty-first century and to redefine how we add value to our lives.

Recall that there are now half as many cell phones in the world as human inhabitants. However you slice it, that's a great milestone—but it still means at least half do not have cell phones, and from some of the estimates I've seen, three-quarters of the world's inhabitants do not have immediate access to telecommunications of any kind. What about the great ideas trapped in those minds?

*If any theme is consistent throughout human history, it is this silly notion that we have finally figured it out.*

Nicholas Negroponte's One Laptop Per Child initiative to put a computer into the hands of every child in developing countries, Mark Bent's BoGo solar-powered light to bring illumination to the world's remotest villages, the Doctors Without Borders program to bring medical care to areas where no else will—these are the ultimate derivatives of an innovation culture.

Years ago a much more energetic and control-obsessed version of myself asked Peter Drucker a question. We were having lunch, and Peter was sharing with me the perils of getting old, the price of wisdom. It was a good time to share my own failings of youth. So I asked him, "Why is it that despite all of the work and writing I do to analyze, describe, and shape organizational behavior, I still find it so amazingly difficult to follow my own prescriptions?"

Peter looked at me with slight disdain and said, "You take yourself far too seriously, Tom. Don't try so hard."

Coming from the world's greatest workaholic that was odd advice. But as I've aged, the words increasingly make more sense. Peter's comments had nothing to do with how hard or how much we work but instead were an observation on how much we convince ourselves how much we truly have achieved.

It seems that most of us take not only ourselves but our collective achievements far too seriously. It's not that we should dismiss what has been accomplished but rather that we should learn to let go, just a little bit, of the notion that we have it all figured out.

If any theme is consistent throughout human history (or any one human's history), it is this silly notion that we have finally figured it out. We like the arrogance of placing ourselves, our generation, our technology, our time and our place in history at the end of the story. History should teach us that we are always in the middle of the story, always stumbling over new chapters that make obsolete much of what has already been written.

*We desperately want to believe that we've cracked the code, but that limits our ability to innovate beyond—and out of—our current circumstances.*

The newness of each trend, technology, and terror we face seems to infatuate us as the latest and greatest of its kind. If age bestows any lasting benefit it is the realization that too often we dress old problems in new clothes and expect them to behave differently. As a parent, I can assure you it doesn't work that way.

We have a lot of work to do, and so do our children. Consider this:

- We find ourselves giddy over the use of the Internet, yet by even the most optimistic measure less than 20 percent of the world's population can use it.

- We talk about a flat world, yet three out of four people still don't have personal access to a telephone.

- Two-thirds of the world's inhabitants form the base of the economic pyramid, with yearly incomes of less than $3,000.

Don't get me wrong, I'm anything but a pessimist. I believe deeply that we are moving forward and that getting technology in the hands of everyone is a big part of that. I just worry that we will give ourselves too much credit and not enough motivation to keep moving forward.

Urban legend has it that in 1899 Charles H. Duell, commissioner of the U.S. Patent Office, said, "Everything that can be invented has been invented." While nobody has ever confirmed Duell's quote, most of us can imagine it being said, especially at a time that was so rich in invention that it might well have seemed as though all of mankind's secrets had been discovered. It's human nature that we desperately want to believe that we've cracked the code. It raises our esteem and fuels our egos. But the unfortunate side effect of this attitude is that we diminish our ability to think outside what we know and limit our ability to innovate beyond—and out of—our current circumstances.

Over time most people come to the conclusion that great inventions and great inventors are either super-smart or super-lucky, and somehow they happen to be at the right place at the right time.

The way many of us look at innovation is focused on invention because our attention has been captured by the human icons of invention. Our fascination with invention probably began as young children. In my case I had a terrible fear about the future. Infatuated as I was by the great legacy of inventors before me, from Ford and Marconi to Carnegie and DuPont, I was convinced that everything good had already been created. I was terrified that in the future invention would be much harder than it was in the past. After all, how difficult was it to sit under a tree and watch an apple fall and then come up with the notion of gravity, or to build a lightbulb, or to catch a lightning bolt with a kite? The thought of how easy these early inventors had it haunted me for years.

I would lie awake at night, my mind racing, thinking of things I could invent. But inevitably most everything I came up with already existed. I'd lament and think to myself, "If only I had been born a few hundred years ago."

Such were the ruminations of a youngster infatuated with the idea of discovery and invention, a youngster who could never have conceived of the rich and extraordinary list of great discoveries that would occur during his lifetime.

Over the years the bright-eyed creativity of youth was pushed aside, replaced by risk assessment, rationality, return on investment, predictability. Yet, like so many others, I continued to look on with amazement at the way an occasional idea had the capacity to change the world, and I marveled, in awe and reverence, at the power behind innovation.

*Every test you ever took measured how well you understood the past, not how well you could create the future.*

Let it go. You are an innovator and you need to be an innovator. You are creative and you are capable of innovation. It's just that no one ever taught you how to innovate. In fact, just the opposite has occurred. You've been taught how to stifle and suppress innovation in favor of predictable results. Every test you ever took measured how well you understood the past, not how well you could create the future. The rigor of an outdated model of research and development and the discipline of hard science has placed the vast majority of us well outside the Innovation Zone.

I hope this book has shown you that innovation is relatively straightforward to do once you know how and once you are part of an organization and a process that encourages and supports it. So if it's that easy, why isn't everyone doing it? Well, I said it was straightforward, but I didn't say it was without risk and challenge. Swinging from a trapeze is straightforward once you know how, but it never gets safe. There is always risk, fear, and trepidation when you swing out on a rope sixty feet above the ground. The same goes for innovation.

Innovation is about moving forward with faith in the fact that one foot will follow the other. Go ahead, take that first step. The world needs innovators like you!

# APPENDIX

## WHAT'S YOUR INNOVATION NUMBER?

### *An Innovation Self-Assessment*

Ten years ago when I began looking at the behaviors and capabilities needed to sustain innovation, I decided to develop an assessment instrument that would help me better understand how organizations perceived their own capability. As part of my work with hundreds of organizations over that time I've been able to administer and refine that assessment. The overall assessment includes seventy specific questions and metrics.

The assessment that follows provides insight into a number of the core metrics and will help you better understand some of the areas where your own organization has inherent innovation strengths and weaknesses. Before you read about others' responses and the insights, I suggest that you take a few minutes to fill out your own Innovation Capability Test, on the following pages. Then compare your answers to those from the aggregate responses of the three hundred companies that have already taken the Innovation Capability Test. While the information here offers only a slice of the overall picture in terms of the subset of questions and the fact that it only compares your perspective, not that of a cross section of your organization, you'll still find that the comparison provides a sense of where your organization stands.

# INNOVATION CAPABILITY TEST

## SECTION A: DEFINING INNOVATION

**1. In your experience, which of the following best describes the sort of innovation you have been part of?** *(Check only one.)*

a. ___ A radical new product

b. ___ A radical new process

c. ___ An incremental change in a customer-facing product or process

d. ___ A refinement of a backroom process

e. ___ A new way of thinking about the organization (a new vision or strategy)

f. ___ Don't know

**2. Can innovation be measured?** *(Again, rely on experience and check only one.)*

a. ___ Innovation cannot be measured

b. ___ Innovation can sometimes be measured

c. ___ Innovation can always be measured

d. ___ Don't know

## SECTION B: INNOVATION TOOLS AND METHODS

**3. What are three different tools you use in practice to foster innovative thinking?** *(Add more if you wish; leave blank if you are not aware of three such tools.)*

a. _____

b. _____

c. _____

**4. Which of the following does your organization use to help promote innovation?** *(Check all that apply.)*

a. ___ Innovation management

b. ___ Knowledge management

c. ___ Incentives for new inventions

d. __ Training on innovative thinking

e. __ Scientific methods for innovation

f. __ None

g. __ Don't know

## SECTION C: LEARNING INNOVATION

**5. Do you believe that innovation can be taught? Why or why not?** *(Write your brief response.)*

_____

_____

_____

_____

**6. Have you ever taken a formal course (academic or corporate) dedicated to innovation or creative problem solving?** *(Check one.)*
__ Yes    __ No

## SECTION D: OPENNESS IN INNOVATION

**7. If a new idea emerges in your company outside the ranks of executive management, how would you characterize its likelihood of making it into practice?** *(Check only one.)*

a. __ Very likely

b. __ Somewhat likely

c. __ Unlikely

d. __ Very unlikely

e. __ Don't know

**8. Think of the last good idea you had to add value to your organization. What happened to it?** *(Check only one.)*

a. __ I lost interest in championing it due to internal process and bureaucracy

b. __ It did not make it past a review committee (but it was reviewed)

c. __ I had no idea what to do with it, so it just languished

d. __ It was embraced by an executive sponsor and was put to use

e. ___ It was reviewed by a committee and put to use

f. ___ I just bulldozed it through all obstacles and it was put to use

g. ___ I just went ahead with it and it was put to use

h. ___ Other (or N/A)

## SECTION E: INTERNAL AND EXTERNAL AWARENESS

**9. How would you rank your company's internal awareness, based on how well you know and can quickly access the right resources, capabilities, knowledge, and talent inside your company?** *(Check only one.)*

___ Poor       ___ Fair      ___ Average      ___ Good      ___ Excellent

**10. How would you rank your company's internal responsiveness, based on how quickly and effectively you can coordinate resources, capabilities, knowledge, and talent into a team and project?** *(Check only one.)*

___ Poor       ___ Fair      ___ Average      ___ Good      ___ Excellent

**11. How would you rank your company's external responsiveness, based on how quickly and effectively you can bring the results of a new team or project to the market?** *(Check only one.)*

___ Poor       ___ Fair      ___ Average      ___ Good      ___ Excellent

**12. How would you rank your company's external awareness, based on how quickly and how well you can sense the market's response to your new product service and re-internalize it?** *(Check only one.)*

___ Poor       ___ Fair      ___ Average      ___ Good      ___ Excellent

# Comparing Your Innovation Capability

Now you can take a look at your responses to the Innovation Capability Test and how your answers compare with those of other organizations. Keep in mind that this is just a small subset of questions from the full assessment.

**QUESTION 1: In your experience, which of the following best describes the sort of innovation you have been part of?**

Organizations overwhelmingly experience innovation as a new vision or strategy, while 27 percent indicate that innovation is part of creating a radical new product or process. Another 20 percent experience innovation as an incremental change in a product or process.

The responses to this question point to a broad set of innovation experiences. The key here is that innovation must be more than a product agenda; it must also play a continuous role in all aspects of a business. This reflects an attitude toward innovation as a systemic approach rather than as a periodic or cyclical phenomenon.

**How to rate your answer:**

A = 10,  B = 20,  C = 5,  D = 5,  E = 30,  F = –5

TOTAL = _____

**Question 1 Response**

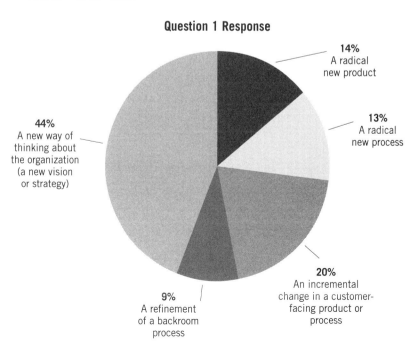

14%
A radical
new product

13%
A radical
new process

44%
A new way of
thinking about
the organization
(a new vision
or strategy)

20%
An incremental
change in a customer-
facing product or
process

9%
A refinement
of a backroom
process

### QUESTION 2: Can innovation be measured?

One of the most powerful insights had to do with measuring innovation. An overwhelming 92 percent of respondents indicated that innovation could be measured—at least sometimes—with 27 percent saying it could always be measured. This is encouraging, as it counters the popular notion that innovation is not something for which investment can be justified. It's reasonable to expect that this more positive perception will fuel the move toward specific innovation projects and initiatives, but it's also clear that there is a fair amount of ambivalence around innovation metrics.

When you probe the respondents who fall into the "sometimes" category, what you find is that they would like to measure innovation but do not know how. The most straightforward approaches are the ways described in the section on innovation velocity in chapter 7 or documenting the flow of ideas through the "Path from Invention to Innovation Funnel" (see Figure 2 on p. 22). Both provide a hard metric of the volume, flow, and impact of innovation. Without these in place it is highly unlikely that any innovation process can be measured over a sustained period of time.

**How to rate your answer:**

A = –10,  B = 20,  C = 50,  D = –5

TOTAL = _____

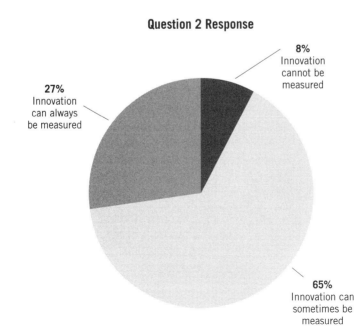

**Question 2 Response**

8%
Innovation cannot be measured

27%
Innovation can always be measured

65%
Innovation can sometimes be measured

**QUESTION 3: What are three different tools you use in practice to foster innovative thinking?**

How quickly did you come up with the tools you listed for this question? The overwhelming answer for most people is *brainstorming*. From there responses drop off dramatically. However, myriad tools and methods have been around for many years to assist in fostering innovative thinking, such as Morphological Matrix, Mind Mapping, and Hits and Hot Spots. The value of the response is the number of distinct approaches you can define.

**How to rate your answer:**

Give yourself 5 points for each response you provided up to a maximum of 25 points.

TOTAL = _____

### Question 3 Responses

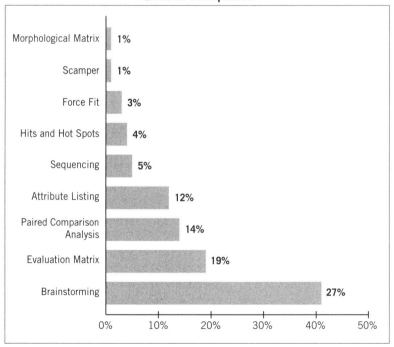

**QUESTION 4: Which of the following does your organization use to help promote innovation?**

As pointed out in this book, innovation does not just happen; it needs constant promotion and mechanisms to facilitate the process of involvement on the part of employees to submit new ideas and to filter and build those ideas into value. This question looks at how an organization approaches that process.

Not surprisingly, the majority of organizations do it through systems already in place to promote the capture and sharing of intellectual property, which are most often their existing knowledge management systems. These may be formal or informal approaches that use basic technology to share ideas and enable collaboration or even less sophisticated methods of frequent socialization, such as coffee hours or group brainstorming sessions.

Far fewer rely on an innovation management system by name. These can be sophisticated home-grown or off-the-shelf technology solutions that provide a platform throughout the life cycle of the innovation to track ideas as they mature and ultimately add measurable value.

Incentives are also frequently used to motivate employees to come up with ideas and to be rewarded based on their value to the organization. It should be mentioned here that the incentives are most often not direct monetary rewards; they are more likely to be part of an overall recognition program that also includes some sort of balanced scorecard, which includes an innovation metric as a way of assessing an employee's performance.

Training is just as important in developing a skill base and an appreciation of the value process has in innovation, and a fair amount of this is reflected in the responses—but not as much as might be expected given the emphasis innovation has been getting in many organizations. When you discuss these responses you find that the problem is in most cases the same as that of innovation management in that there are not yet many options for innovation-specific training from either an academic or professional development standpoint.

Perhaps the most interesting aspect of the responses to this question were the 10 percent who responded that they had either no means of promoting innovation or didn't know how they promoted it. There is nothing particularly telling in the demographic of these responses that might cause them to not need to promote innovation (that is, they are not all government agencies). So the only conclusion is that there are indeed many organizations that do not actively promote innovation in any way. A frightening thought, but one that speaks to the nascent nature of the topic.

### How to rate your answer:

Give yourself the points shown for each answer you provided. Sum the points for each answer to get your total ranking for this question.

A = 25,  B = 15,  C = 50,  D = 35,  E = 25,  F or G = –10

TOTAL = _____

## Question 4 Aggregate Response

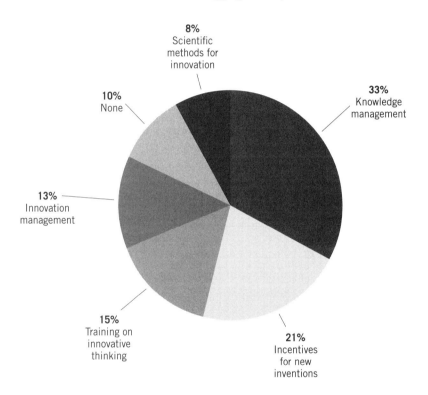

8%
Scientific
methods for
innovation

10%
None

33%
Knowledge
management

13%
Innovation
management

15%
Training on
innovative
thinking

21%
Incentives
for new
inventions

### QUESTION 5: Do you believe that innovation can be taught?

This is a telling question since it cuts to the fundamental issues behind instilling a culture of innovation in any organization. If the belief that innovation is a teachable skill does not exist, then it will be an uphill battle to introduce it in any systemic way. That doesn't mean it's impossible—only that it will take significantly longer and require a much higher level of risk and therefore leadership initiative. This appears to be the case in 19 percent of all organizations across industries. Fortunately 81 percent of organizations do believe that innovation is a trainable skill. It is also interesting to note that the demographic of the 19 percent is representative of the more tenured (read older) respondents. This too is not surprising, but it does present an obstacle to be considered since this 19 percent represents the power base in many organizations.

**How to rate your answer:**

Innovation can be taught = 25

Innovation can't be taught = −25

TOTAL = _____

**Question 5 Response**

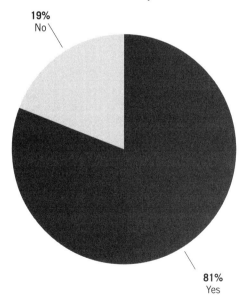

19%
No

81%
Yes

### QUESTION 6: Have you ever taken a formal course (academic or corporate) dedicated to innovation or creative problem solving?

Given the large number of affirmative responses to question 5, you might expect that question 6 would look a bit different than it does. Instead, there is a fairly even split between respondents who have taken any sort of innovation training and those who have not. There is also no significant correlation between the two questions. This means that some people who have been trained still think it's not a teachable skill and some who haven't been trained believe it is. Again this seems to speak more to the predisposition of the person than the efficacy of the training process. But the more interesting aspect of this is that of the 44 percent who have been trained, the amount of training is negligible, with a very small number (less than 10 percent) having had training of more than one day.

### How to rate your answer:

You have taken a formal course on innovation or creative problem solving = 25

You have not taken a formal course on innovation or creative problem solving = –25

Give yourself an extra 10 points if your course lasted longer than one day.

TOTAL = _____

**Question 6 Response**

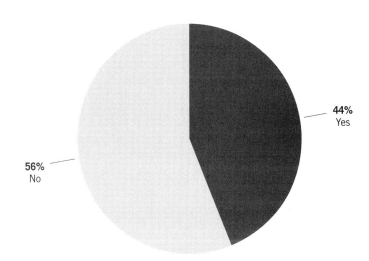

44%
Yes

56%
No

**QUESTION 7: If a new idea emerges in your company outside the ranks of executive management, how would you characterize its likelihood of making it into practice?**

This question is striking in the contrast between the "Very likely" response and all other possible outcomes. While it may appear on the surface that this is a natural distribution, since not all ideas are good ideas and therefore not all will make it into practice, the question is a bellwether for the way ideas are treated in an organization.

What the question illustrates is both the likelihood that an idea is both likely to have value (that is, do employees understand what ideas are most likely to add value to the business and the market) as well as the way the organization collects and filters ideas. When comparisons are conducted between specific organizations that answer this question, those who respond "Very likely" consistently rank higher in all other aspects of their Innovation Capability as well, while those who respond "Somewhat likely" or "Very unlikely" rate consistently lower on their Innovation Capability.

**How to rate your answer:**

A = 25,  B = 10,  C = –20,  D = –35,  E = –15

TOTAL = _____

### Question 7 Response

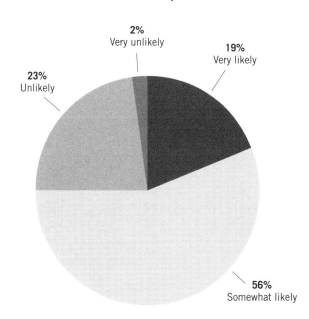

2%
Very unlikely

19%
Very likely

23%
Unlikely

56%
Somewhat likely

**QUESTION 8: Think of the last good idea you had to add value to your organization. What happened to it?**

If 19 percent of respondents indicated that an idea was very unlikely to make it into practice, it is not surprising that 29 percent of respondents also felt that their idea had not made it into practice as the result of falling into one of the top four categories in this question. However, the more interesting aspect of this question is what actually happens to ideas that do and don't make it through.

In the case of those ideas that did not make it into practice, only 6 percent were actually reviewed in any fashion. The remainder (23 percent) languished, lost the interest of the originator, or followed their originator to another company. That is a startling observation. Were these ideas to all die in a committee review, at least we could say there is a process in place by which to evaluate them and determine value, but the vast majority never get that far—a testament to the lack of innovation processes in most companies.

In the case of those that did make it through, only 10 percent were again reviewed by a committee. The rest found favor in the eyes of an executive or simply ended up being bulldozed or plowed through the organization. While it's tempting to say that this is adequate as long as the idea comes to fruition, it is also a very haphazard way to treat innovation. It relies on a brute force method that values ideas based on how stubborn the idea's owner is, but this is not an indicator of how good the idea is and does nothing to foster the submission of good ideas by less disruptive and bullheaded individuals.

I call responses in the "Just went ahead with it" and "Bulldozed it through" categories as the Yellow Zone, meaning that they are of concern as indicators that a system is not in place to manage innovation. Responses in the "I lost interest," "It will probably end up in the next company I join/start," or "It just languished" categories are in what I call the Red Zone, meaning that the organization is creating antibodies that actually attack and suppress innovation. Staying out of the danger zones requires systems that offer a safe haven for ideas.

**How to rate your answer:**

Other = 0

It was embraced by an executive sponsor = 10

It made it through committee = 20

I just went ahead with it = 5

I bulldozed it through = 5

I lost interest = –10

It will probably end up in the next company I join/start = –10

It just languished = –10

It didn't pass review committee (but it was reviewed) = 20

TOTAL = _____

### Question 8 Response

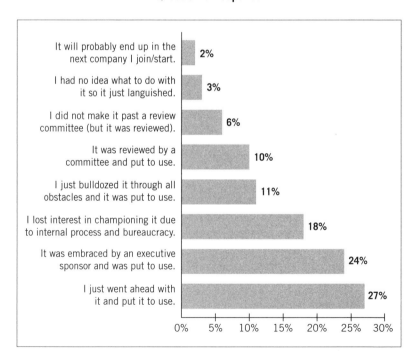

# Your Own Innovation Rating

**QUESTIONS 9 through 12**

These questions do not have much relevance from a comparative stand-point in looking at how you rate against other organizations. Instead they illustrate where you perceive your internal collective strengths and weaknesses regarding innovation. What is relevant in these questions is how the perception of strengths and weaknesses changes across the four quadrants of the innovation chain we discussed earlier.

To understand the significance of your responses, you need to plot them side by side as shown in the chart below. In this example (only a sample), the organization exhibits a bell curve shifted to the right. This reflects an organization that is fairly progressive in its innovation capability.

### Questions 9–12 Sample

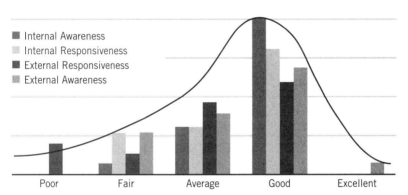

Organizations with the greatest difficulty with innovation as a process are those that tend to have an overall bell curve for all bars that shifts to the left of the chart (Poor–Good) and favors Internal quadrants over External quadrants. This is typical of an organization that is entrenched in a mar-ket and far less likely to change its processes or products quickly enough to address new opportunities, organically or through acquisitions. Organizations that shift to the right (Fair–Excellent) in their External quadrants are most often midsize organizations that may be challenged internally by scale but still have a keen sense of the market.

Smaller organizations are the ones who find themselves shifting to the right side of the chart in all categories. However, there are notable exceptions to this. Companies that consistently sustain innovation most closely resemble the profile of a small company, nimble in both internal and external areas as well as in awareness and responsiveness. These are organizations that have been able to retain an entrepreneurial spirit and have put in place systems that allow them to counteract the inertia of scale, whether organically or through acquisition.

**How to rate your answers:**
Assign points based on where the peak of your bell curve was for each category as shown in the table below.

## SCORING QUESTIONS 9–12

|  | Poor | Fair | Average | Good | Excellent | Score |
|---|---|---|---|---|---|---|
| **9. Internal Awareness** | −10 | −5 | 0 | 5 | 10 | |
| **10. Internal Responsiveness** | −10 | −5 | 0 | 5 | 10 | |
| **11. External Responsiveness** | −10 | −5 | 0 | 5 | 10 | |
| **12. External Awareness** | −10 | −5 | 0 | 5 | 10 | |

TOTAL = _____

# Your Overall Score

Add up the total lines for your responses to the twelve questions. You should have a grand total between –160 and 360. Here is what your total means.

### NEGATIVE (<0) RANKING

If you are in the negative range (less than 0), then I'm grateful that you even considered reading a book on innovation, although you may very well have had to hide it out of sight—if you even dared bring it to your workplace. Your organization clearly has some serious work to do across many aspects of how you put in place processes for innovation.

Problems that are typical in these sorts of organizations are lack of leadership, a mature marketplace with little room for differentiation, a strong focus on operational excellence due to heavy pressure on cost cutting and financial restructuring, or simply a declining business model. Momentum against innovation may well be so entrenched that nothing short of a catastrophe can reshape the organization. If you're going to stick it out, look for ways to create quick successes, no matter how small, to demonstrate how an innovative approach can jump-start a fresh approach. Then again, it may be time to consider better options. All organizations have a life cycle, and without a significant change in leadership and business model the ultimate fate of poor innovation is no different in business than it is in nature: extinction.

### NEUTRAL (0–100) RANKING

The good news is you have lots of company if your score fell in this range. Most organizations have some basis and experience in innovation and have acknowledged the importance of innovation in the organization. The bad news is that you may not have used innovation as much as you can or should. You probably have pockets of exceptional innovative capacity and many very successful products, services, and processes. But it is likely that they are disconnected from each other by scale or geography or systems and management techniques. With a focused effort in these it is very likely that you could quickly move to the next level. These efforts would require putting in place a platform to connect people and help them better mine ideas while also managing these ideas as they surface. If the right leadership is in place, then keep moving forward to build momentum behind innovation.

## POSITIVE (101–250) RANKING

You're well ahead of the curve. It looks as though you already have a strong culture in place with visible leadership behind the innovation initiatives in your organization. Scaling your innovation efforts may be an issue, but there is no absolute scale regarding innovation. You may be well off in the context of your industry and the constraints you have, which require you to balance risk with innovation. For example, in many regulated industries innovation is unfortunately limited by the external constraints imposed on the processes, marketing, and evaluation of ideas. However, this doesn't mean you can't improve the degree to which your organization fosters internal mechanisms for rewarding new ideas in a variety of areas that are not in conflict with regulated aspects of the business. My own experience with organizations that fall into this range is that they have made an explicit decision that further investment in innovation is just not warranted given the risk it entails. That's a fair assessment, and it may be that this is as far as you need to go at this point! But keep an open mind as the climate of your industry and organization changes.

## STRONG POSITIVE (251+) RANKING

You're either a case study in this book or you should be in the next version. The practices and processes you have in place foster a culture and set of systems for sustaining innovation. This hasn't happened overnight, nor has it been accidental. Your leadership, values, brand perception, and rewards are all built around a solid foundation and practical approach to innovation. This is part of the fiber of your company and how you mentor and train new employees as well as partners and even perhaps customers.

Congratulations, you are leading the charge into the future and acting as a role model for what innovation should be. Don't be bashful—the world needs to hear your story and learn from your success.

Or perhaps you are the CEO or a senior executive and just answered the way you wished your organization was, in which case I applaud your vision. Now get back to reality and make it happen! You know what needs to be done.

# NOTES

## Introduction

1. Tamar Lewin, "U.S. Universities Rush to Set Up Outposts Abroad," *New York Times,* February 10, 2008.

## Chapter 1

1. Organisation for Economic Co-operation and Development (OECD), *Encyclopedia Britannica,* 2008. Available online by subscription, Encyclopedia Britannica Online: www.britannica.com/eb/article-9031928. Access date: June 30, 2008.
2. Glenn Mangurian, "Realizing What You're Made Of," *Harvard Business Review* (March 2007).
3. Stefan Wuchty, Benjamin F. Jones, and Brian Uzzi, "The Increasing Dominance of Teams in Production of Knowledge," *Science* 316 (May 18, 2007): 1036–1039.
4. Jeff Weedman, vice president of licensing and corporate new ventures, Procter & Gamble, from a presentation at the Yet2.com Executive Briefing Conference, Boston, November 6–8, 2007.
5. Partners HealthCare, 2007 Annual Report.

## Chapter 2

1. The Partners HealthCare case was developed by the author for the Center for Business Innovation, which he leads at Babson College Executive Education. Used with permission from Babson College.
2. Partners HealthCare, 2007 Annual Report.

## Chapter 3

1. Alfred P. Sloan, *My Years with General Motors* (New York: Doubleday, 1964), 177.
2. Henry Chesbrough and David Tecce, "When Is Virtual Virtuous? Organizing for Innovation," *Harvard Business Review* (January–February 1996): 67.

## Chapter 4

1. Numerous books have been written about how the longitude problem was solved. One of the best is Dava Sobel's *Longitude: The True Story of a Lone Genius Who Solved the Greatest Problem of His Time* (New York: Penguin, 1996).

## Chapter 5

1. The term was coined by Henry Chesbrough in his book *Open Innovation* (Boston: Harvard Business School Press, 2003).
2. Jeff Howe, "The Rise of Crowdsourcing," *Wired* 14, no. 6 (June 2006).
3. "At P&G It's '360 Degree Innovation,'" interview with P&G CTO Gilbert Cloyd, *BusinessWeek,* October 11, 2004.

## Chapter 6

1. Rajshree Agarawl and Michael Gort, "Consumer and Products Goods," *Journal of Law & Economics* 44 (April 2001).
2. Steve Diller, Nathan Shedroff, and Darrel Rhea, *Making Meaning: How Successful Businesses Deliver Meaningful Customer Experiences* (Upper Saddle River, NJ: New Riders Press, 1995).

## Chapter 7

1. Portions of the Johnson Controls example excerpted with permission from a case study developed by MindMatter, Inc.

## Chapter 8

1. Statistics from Anthony Carnevale, Educational Testing Service, "The Future of Education, Employment and Training Policy," presentation at an American Youth Policy forum, Washington, DC, July 27, 2001; summarized online at www.aypf.org/forumbriefs/2001/fb072701.htm. Note that the number cited for college-educated workers to enter the workforce by 2020—49 million—is perhaps generous. Estimates by the National Center for Public Policy & Higher Education predict a net reduction in college-educated workers by 2020 (*BusinessWeek,* November 21, 2005).
2. See Hernandoto Desoto, *The Mystery of Capital: Why Capitalism Triumphs in the West and Fails Everywhere Else* (New York: Basic Books, 2000).

# INDEX